She
Takes on the
World

**A GUIDE TO BEING YOUR OWN BOSS,
WORKING HAPPY, AND LIVING
ON PURPOSE**

NATALIE MACNEIL

INFINITY
PUBLISHING

Note from the author: Some names have been changed in this book to protect the privacy of the individuals involved.

ISBN 978-0-7414-7187-1 Paperback
ISBN 978-0-7414-7188-8 Hardcover
ISBN 978-0-7414-7194-9 Audio book
ISBN 978-0-7414-7213-7 eBook

Printed in the United States of America

Published January 2012

INFINITY PUBLISHING
1094 New DeHaven Street, Suite 100
West Conshohocken, PA 19428-2713
Toll-free (877) BUY BOOK
Local Phone (610) 941-9999
Fax (610) 941-9959
Info@buybooksontheweb.com
www.buybooksontheweb.com

TO THE RISK-TAKERS,
CHANGE AGENTS, DREAMERS, DOERS,
AND ALL-AROUND PASSIONATE WOMEN
TAKING ON THE WORLD:

This book is for you.

Table of Contents

··
CHAPTER 2
··

··
CHAPTER 3
··

CHAPTER 4

CHAPTER 5

....
CHAPTER 6
....

....
CHAPTER 7
....

CHAPTER 8

CHAPTER 9

CHAPTER 10

CHAPTER 11

Welcome

TO A WHOLE NEW WORLD

IT'S A WOMAN'S WORLD

WOMEN OF THE WORLD, I am speaking to you. Not from a platform of unreachable heights, but from my heart, standing right beside you.

There has never been a better time than now to make the final break with outdated traditions in the business world. As old paradigms fade, new opportunities, methods, paths and successes are springing up all around you. Open your mind and your eyes will follow.

The Great Recession turned the economy upside down. While corporate jobs were being lost, new small businesses sprouted up at a phenomenal rate as people created their own streams of income. According to the Intuit 2020 Report, contingent workers will make up over 40 percent of the total workforce by 2020, with the greatest growth found in personal and micro-businesses.[1]

Whether you were born an entrepreneur or found your way into self-employment out of necessity, there are more of us than ever before, and we have the power to change the world.

We're living in a new era. And after years spent following the lead of men, climbing our way up the ladder, and hammering at the glass ceiling, it's women who are leading the way as the dominant economic force.

Yes — welcome to the Sheconomy!

Would it surprise you to learn that Gen-Y women are enrolling in and graduating from college at a higher rate than men? Women make up half of the workforce, and we are creating new businesses at twice the rate of our male counterparts.

What excites me the most about there being more women entrepreneurs is that we have an opportunity to lead differently and shape a better world. A study by the Guardian Life Small Business Research Institute shows that women are more likely to include community and the environment in business plans, are committed to creating opportunities for the people around them, and care deeply about paying employees well and providing better healthcare.[2]

This is only one small glimpse into the values and ideas we may sow into the Sheconomy.

We are at the beginning of a revolution, the biggest shift since women charged into the workforce. It's a movement that is bigger than any *one* of us. It's an exciting time to be a woman!

WHAT BURIED PASSION IS WAITING TO EMERGE?

DID YOU HAVE A DREAM early in life that was stifled or submerged by classical schooling and cultural "norms?" It's not uncommon, and with all due respect to society and its childhood institutions, the typical path can be quite lacking in its capacity to cultivate creativity and vision.

This is one reason why decades later, so many women find themselves in roles they didn't choose, or that don't match their early dreams and passions.

Institutional dream-crushing started for me at the tender age of 13, when a few middle school teachers started insisting that my childhood dream of being an "entrepreneur-author-teacher-speaker-astronaut" was quite positively out of the question.

This probably happened to you, too. Once it does, you are herded down an ever-narrowing tunnel of "opportunities" with the rest of your unsuspecting classmates. Each tunnel is labeled with its own pleasant archetype and the steps you must take to get to the end.

It used to be that women who showed interest in the medical field were often led down the tunnel labeled "nursing," whereas a male in the same situation would be expected to walk down the one labeled "doctor."

Make no mistake, these were predetermined, designed, well-trodden paths where your interests took a back seat to your "career."

Sure, you got a few "choices" along the way, like where you wanted to get your diploma, but really, the rest was pretty much standard procedure.

I was guided down the "lawyer" tunnel. I clearly remember sitting in front of my computer, eagerly awaiting the results of my "best career choice" from a personal inventory software program. I was secretly hoping the result would be CEO or entrepreneur. My aunt and uncle were business owners, and I wanted to own companies like they did.

When the software program spat out LAWYER, my heart sank a little. I told myself, "Well, the computer probably knows what's best," and I resigned myself to becoming a lawyer right then and there.

Through movies like *Legally Blonde*, I tried to convince myself that life as a lawyer could be fun because, of course, *Legally Blonde* is such a realistic depiction of a career in law... I thought I could still honor the entrepreneur in me by starting my own firm. "Yeah, it won't be that bad," I remember thinking.

I earned good grades and decided to go after the logical degree, Business and Political Science. Nobody stopped me. No one questioned my thought process. No one talked to me about entrepreneurship being a viable option for me.

They should have. There is sunshine at the end of that tunnel, however. In hindsight, I learned one of my first and most valuable lessons:

**ONLY YOU KNOW WHAT IS IN YOUR HEART.
NEVER LET SOMEONE ELSE TELL YOU WHAT YOU LOVE.
MORE IMPORTANTLY, DON'T LET THE PRESSURE
OF EXPECTATIONS DICTATE HOW YOU LIVE.**

Be your own person, listen to your inner voice, and vigilantly stand guard at the door of your own mind. No one loves you more than you do. Be a good gatekeeper — your life depends on it!

LEMONADE STAND DREAMS

SO WHAT DID *you* WANT TO DO before you were rubber-stamped and sent down the assembly line? Sadly, for many people, it's not what they are doing today.

Back when my seven-year-old self dreamed of being an "entrepreneur-author-teacher-speaker-astronaut," I tried my hand at the tycoon-making business of running a Grade A lemonade stand with a capital investment from my mom and dad.

I know, I know, a lemonade stand is not the most original idea. It's what it taught me that makes the experience extraordinary and memorable.

Perception and attitude are amazing gifts, and they make us all different. If you interviewed one hundred children who tried running lemonade stands and asked them what they learned and experienced, I bet you would get one hundred unique stories. The setting and plot might be the same, but the journey, obstacles and outcomes would be vastly different.

What I learned were the basics of business. I interacted with my customers, listening to their suggestions and desires, always caring if they were happy. I developed marketing materials: signs, colors, cup choices and sales pitches. I kept track of my revenue and expenses, always making sure I did not overstock and leaving enough to buy more product the next weekend.

Last of all, earning well over my allowance, I began to learn about the value of money.

After crowning myself "Lemonade Queen," I used my knowledge and imagination to expand past ordinary sugared lemon water into new and unexplored territories: fruit punch, popsicles, and cookies! Some products did well, while others weren't worth the time my assistant (a. k.a. mom) and I spent on them.

How simple these lessons seem now. Learning to simplify your life again so that you can hear and absorb lessons is a compulsory part of reinvention. You have more courage and power than you think; give yourself the environment to remember that.

LESSONS AND CONFESSIONS:
Melody Biringer on Knowing Yourself

Growing up on my family's strawberry farm culti-vated an enterprising spirit in me from early on.

I was so excited to get out there with all the older kids and work my own berry row to start making my first buck. Well, I lasted one day. Picking strawberries was the worst job you could possibly have, I thought. There had to be a better way.

I looked out across the strawberry fields at all those hard-working berry pickers and inspiration hit me. I begged my dad to borrow a few bucks, and I rode my bike to the little store down the road and bought up all the lemonade. I set up shop the next day and started my first real money-making venture: selling lemonade to the berry pickers!

I really don't know how or why I thought like this at eight years old, but a day later I hired my cousins to run the operation for me. I paid back the money I bor-rowed from my dad, paid my employees, and I reveled in my business savvy. Holding all that green cash in my pink little palms — cash that I'd earned all by myself — started me on a life-long love affair with makin' a buck.

> **LESSON LEARNED:** *Know thyself. At eight years old, I knew that I wanted to do things my way. With every business endeavor, I have been able to quickly understand that when something agitates me, that's my cue to flip that agitation into opportunity. I love the hunt for the fix because for me, it just reeks of buck-building potential.*
>
> — Melody Biringer
>
> Founder, *The CRAVE Company*

LIFE AND TIMES OF A STUDENT

COLLEGE WAS AN INTERESTING JOURNEY FOR ME. Like many of my peers, I had no real sense of reward for what I was doing. I was basically just following the Pied Piper to the edge of the towering cliffs of education. We were all prepared to jump, in unison, to the death of our dreams and freedoms; bodies piling on bodies, scraping and clawing at each other to begin our journey in the rat race like so many generations before us.

Okay, maybe it wasn't quite that dramatic, but it's not too far a stretch.

To make matters worse, I found myself working a less-than-glamorous summer job at a car factory. It was my first taste of working full-time for someone else and I didn't like it. It paid my tuition, though, and I didn't need student loans; one potential disaster diverted!

What disturbed me about my job was the empty looks on many of the faces of my co-workers. They seemed absolutely numb. I found myself surrounded by passionless automatons, doing repetitive jobs they hated doing, and literally counting down the years, days, and hours to retirement.

I thought, "So this is where imagination comes to die."

Being surrounded by people who aren't passionate about the work they do can really take a toll on you. They are not alone, though: Only 23 percent of people working for companies are passionate about their jobs, according to one study by Deloitte.[3]

When I was presented with a unique opportunity to go to Asia that autumn with all expenses paid, my inner voice screamed "GO!" I decided to maintain a part-time school schedule through online classes as I puddle-jumped the globe over to Asia and back, then on to Europe, back to North America, then to Africa and back to Europe. Life as a jetsetter was exhilarating, and opened my eyes to a whole new world.

THE WORLD IS YOURS

TRAVELING CHANGED EVERYTHING FOR ME. I saw different cultures. I saw how things could be and how they should never be. I saw that there is more than one way to live and be. And that has made all the difference.

When I first started on my travels I was looking for something — adventure, a purpose, happiness. I found all those things — not in the amazing places I got to visit and the memorable people I met along the way, but within myself.

Have you ever had a really powerful epiphany? I mean a massive a-ha moment, where two thoughts collide in your mind at the speed of light and literally change your world?

Mine was in the Czech Republic. I clearly remember passing a gigantic globe, I'm talking at least two stories high, that read, "THE WORLD IS YOURS." That is when it happened. The air seemed to suck out of my lungs and suspend me for a moment in space. My gut felt punched as images, smells, and thoughts of my seven-year-old "Lemonade Queen" self stood looking at my current self with yearning eyes. "What happened to us?" she seemed to say.

That is when the adrenaline took its second effect and my chest swelled with a courageous and fierce energy. I snatched up my camera and captured that image, hoping to capture as well the feeling and inspiration it had caused.

This moment, this turning point in my life, is where the seed of inspiration was born for *She Takes on the World* (the name later came to me in a dream). I still look at the photo from time to time when I need to be reminded that no dream is too big:

Since that momentous day, I have:

- 🕊 Visited over 60 countries around this big, beautiful planet.

- 🕊 Started a business that was an epic failure.

- 🕊 Started a business, Imaginarius, that is an international success.

❧ Won an EMMY® with my business partner for our work with the National Film Board co-producing the interactive documentary *Out My Window.*[i]

❧ Created *She Takes on the World*, a blog that became one of the top blogs in the world for entrepreneurial women. It was listed by *Forbes.com* on "Top Ten Entrepreneurial Sites for Women" and won the Stevie Award for Blog of the Year.[ii]

❧ Co-founded Y.E.C. Women with bestselling author Scott Gerber, to provide young women with access to tools, mentorship, community and educational resources that support each stage of their businesses' development and growth.

❧ Launched the wildly successful WE Mastermind Product Launch Program with Natalie Sisson.

I have truly found my way back to the "DREAM BIG" mindset my seven-year-old self had. And that's ultimately what taking on the world is all about.

WITHIN THESE PAGES

IT IS MY PASSION TO HELP more women design the career of their dreams. This book is about inspiration, freedom and the audacity to change a predictable, ordinary life into an extraordinary one.

I promise not to bore you with a long diatribe of how oppressed women have been or how hard we have fought through the years for the rights we have today; we've all heard enough of that.

i   EMMY* is a registered trademark of the National Academy of Television Arts & Sciences

ii   Stevie* is a registered trademark of Stevie Awards, Inc.

My business partner, Vincent Marcone, and I with our Emmy Awards.
Photo by Jaime Hogge.

Instead, I'd like to point out that there is still much opportunity to create balance in our culture and worldview. We still compare our salaries with men's to show how much or little we have progressed in equality. There is simply a better way.

You don't have to kick, climb, and claw your way to the top. You don't have to be bitter about being passed over for that big promotion. You don't have to be away from your family working long, stressful hours for not enough pay. You can be your own boss and at the same time, lead us to a better world. There are no limits to what you can achieve when you're in the driver's seat.

If you *are* working for someone else right now, the lessons in this book can still help you power up your career and personal brand. But ask yourself this: "Am I truly fulfilled in my career, or do I need to do some soul-searching to remember my wildest dreams?" I encourage you to explore whether entrepreneurship might be a better path for you. So many women own businesses today, and you can too.

This book is not about coddling you through the startup process — how to register a business, how to pay taxes, how to write an unnecessarily long business plan that you'll never look at again, etc. There are hundreds of viable resources and books out there, a few keystrokes away, to help set up those elements.

What I'm concerned with is guiding you to develop a Master Action Plan (MAP) for our interconnected digital world. Your MAP will help fuse your fiery passion with steadfast purpose, find a niche audience that needs you, build a team to help you grow, and create a thriving business that allows you to live the life you were *meant* to live.

Since there are so many ways to get to a goal, I will focus on absolute necessities, action steps, and most importantly, the mindset it takes to succeed. Once you have the "how," all you need is the courage to take action. The reason it takes courage to act is because the results are undeniable. If we never start, then we never fail. Your mind is the ONLY thing between you and becoming a super-successful entrepreneur.

My hope is that I can gain your trust, enabling you to recognize the insight in these pages and infuse you with the knowledge, power and confidence to make a name for yourself. I'll be by your side as your personal coach and cheerleader.

Bad news travels fast, so I'm sure it's no surprise to you that many reports say that up to 90 percent of small businesses fail in the first year. I am determined to make sure you are not part of that statistic. I can't stress enough how different things are in our digital world, and how many golden opportunities are passed up by women every day.

If you can find your passion, I can help you make it your career. That's a promise.

When I was eight years old, a man across the street named Kevin showed me something called the Internet. I'll never forget him saying, "This is going to be your future, Natalie!" And he was right.

The Internet fascinated me so much that I begged my mom to send me to Engineering Science Camp to learn more about it — and so I went, declaring to my counselor, "I'm here to learn about my future!"

Today, my life is online. I have a virtual business that I can run from anywhere — and I do. Whether you want your business to be completely virtual or not, you can use the online tools I talk about in this book to help you be more productive and streamline your business, so you have more time for the things you love and the people you love.

The changes to the business landscape aren't showing any signs of slowing down. In the last five years alone, we've seen Facebook become a mainstream tool that crosses generations, and Twitter has dominated the real-time sharing of news to give us a never-before-seen point of view on major world events like the revolution in Egypt.

Yes, things have changed — a lot! We need desperately to adapt. Unlike many business and career books, this is a book that reflects the massive changes that have reshaped the business landscape. It is a book for our digital world.

Throughout the book you'll notice some of the following key features:

MASTER ACTION PLAN (MAP) ITEMS

COMPLETE THE ACTION ITEMS in this book to envision your future, prepare for growth, and build your MAP. I'm going to show you how to break down barriers that prevent you from reaching your fullest potential, build a brand that is a reflection of you, and equip you with powerful tools to run a business "in the cloud," giving you the time to enjoy and partake of the most important things in your life — family, travel, social causes, and so on. Most MAP items can be completed right in the book but feel free to use a blank notebook to complete the exercises if you prefer.

LESSONS AND CONFESSIONS

I COLLECTED STORIES from many amazing women throughout the time I spent writing this book. The stories reflect many different stages of the start-up process, as well as the different emotions and thoughts that follow the natural ups and downs of growing a business. You have already heard from powerhouse entrepreneur Melody Biringer of The CRAVE Company, and you'll be hearing from many more women who will hopefully inspire your own growth as an entrepreneur.

NATALIE'S GEMS

WHEN I MENTION SOFTWARE, websites, or tools that I love and use, they will be marked with the 🔷 symbol in the book. All of my "gems" are also listed at the end of the book for your convenience.

IT'S OUR TIME

AS YOU READ, focus on finding your fire. It takes the fire of passion to burn you into action and keep you there.

If you read this book and you still can't decide what your passion is or whether to go for it, write me, Facebook me, or tweet me @nataliemacneil. Do not let your passion slip! Lack of passion is a killer, because it leads to lack of action. And without action, we obviously can't get anywhere.

Devour these pages. If you're a fighter, find something worth fighting for. If you're a lover, find something worth dying for. If you're lost, climb the tallest @ %#ing tree you can and find out where you need to go.

Whatever you do, do not settle. Do not become a passion-less automaton. You were meant for so much more than that.

When you find your fire, don't be afraid to shout it to the world. Passion is infectious. For now, I want you to take a deep breath and get ready to take on the world.

CHAPTER 1

Clearing the Mist:

How to Work Happy and Live on Purpose

THE OBSTACLES IN THE WAY OF WORKING HAPPY

SINCE STARTING *She Takes on the World,* I have been connected to and helped thousands of women in their current careers and businesses. While I don't like to generalize, I have noticed that many women make similar mistakes when starting a business. Hey, I'm guilty of some of them, too!

The problem with a lot of these mistakes is that they end up draining us of our energy and passion for our work, or they leave us with feelings of resentment and bitterness that affect other areas of our lives.

1. **BUSINESS PARTNERS ARE NOT FOR MORAL SUPPORT.** Many of the most successful companies were founded by two or more people, and business partners can truly be a blessing, but you have to think twice about who to go into business with. Women often end up partnering up with a husband or friend, which can be a huge mistake. We're going to come back to this when we talk about choosing a business partner.

2. **DON'T GIVE THE MILK AWAY FOR FREE.** I have found that women tend to give a lot away for free or at too steep a discount. It won't do you any good if you're making less than minimum wage. How will you ever make your clients happy and help others realize their dreams if you are just scraping by? It's

like they tell you in the airplane safety instructions: put your oxygen mask on first, THEN help others!

3. **TOO MANY WOMEN ARE WORKING IN THEIR BUSINESSES, NOT ON THEIR BUSINESSES.** When you delegate and let others work IN your business, you can focus your valuable energy on steering your business forward, increasing revenue, and expanding the reach of your brand. I'll help you build a team later in this book.

4. **NO MATTER HOW MUCH YOU HATE NUMBERS, YOU CAN'T IGNORE THEM IN YOUR BUSINESS.** What was your revenue last month? What were your operating expenses? What salary did you pay yourself? What was your net profit? These are things that will help you to make intelligent decisions instead of educated guesses. To take control of your business finances and get a clear, easy-to-understand picture of your money situation, head to inDinero.com ⬧ right now. It will be one of the best financial decisions you make for your business!

5. **DON'T SETTLE FOR LESS THAN YOUR FULLEST POTENTIAL.** I have to ask too many women, repeatedly, "But what does your business look like in your *wildest* dreams?" Would you believe getting an honest answer is like pulling teeth? It's *okay* to have big, bold dreams. It's okay — and completely realistic — to want to change the world. The confidence, attitude, and determination to back your dreams will follow if you simply have the courage to begin.

6. **WE DON'T HAVE TO BE LIKE MEN TO SUCCEED.** This is at the heart of what *She Takes on the World* is all about. As women, we can succeed by doing things our way. We can shake the business world up by leading differently. I'm always fascinated by women who

think they need to act more like men to succeed. We have innate qualities and powerful leadership skills that the world needs right now. When I interviewed Arianna Huffington, who sold *The Huffington Post* to AOL for $315 million, she had some words of wisdom for women in business: Lead differently, teach the men that there are different paths to success, and let's get some sleep. Amen, Arianna!

THE GOLDEN KEY TO WORKING HAPPY

SUCCESS STARTS WITH LOVE and a passion for what you do. Of course you need a market, too, and people who have a need for your product, but I don't believe in running a business unless you're head-over-heels passionate about it and love what you do.

Passion is your drive and shares a close link with inspiration. Asleep, passion is a smoldering ember; given air it is a white-hot fire. At its most modest, it feels like a gentle pang; at its boldest, it feels like a desperate need.

Passion can burn like a fierce hunger and is your lead foot, pushing the pedal to the metal towards a goal or expectation. It opens doors and lays your path out before you. It's why explorers explore, inventors invent, and painters paint. It is your key to success.

How about love? What do we mean when we say we love what we do? I believe it means we always want to be surrounded by it and be close to it; we feel at ease in its presence. Love calms us when we are nervous and gives us courage where we are weak.

Love leads us around the world, and passion is the boat we travel in. Love is a constant whisper, while passion is a roaring truth. Love is your quiet rock; passion is your fiery spirit. Love is when something becomes a part of you; passion is when you just can't shut up about it.

Love is your ultimate weapon. It truly conquers all and is a formidable foe. It gets you through the tough days you'll inevitably have, like this day I pulled from my journal:

July 15th, 2008

Things are not going as planned. It fucking sucks. I feel like I went into business with the wrong group of people and now I'm carrying the burden of trying to make a failing business work. I don't want to be doing this anymore. I mean, I really love media and it's what I want to be doing and I love my partners as people and I want to have my own business but I think it needs to be MY OWN BUSINESS and not my business that I own with a group of people. I know I can make it on my own and I already have some opportunities I could jump on, but I don't see an easy way of climbing out of the hole I dug myself into.

Yes, that was a low point for me as an entrepreneur as I was watching my first business fail. But I still had a lot of love and passion for the industry, and that love was the bridge that helped me get through that failure and onto my successful business.

Can you imagine how different the world would be if we all loved what we did? How many times have you sat and listened to people bitch and complain about their jobs, but not lift a finger to change their situations?

If you love what you do, you'll have no problem living what you do. In fact, it will just feel natural — second nature.

Now, finding your passion may be easier for some than others, but don't worry. I can help those of you who can't seem to distinguish a passionate feeling from the sensation a pint of chocolate ice cream gives you.

I can also help those who seem to be interested in everything. You know who you are. You endlessly start new projects and then abandon them quickly once you hit a snag or something new and exciting comes along. If you truly love to start things and work best with many "pans on the fire," there is a business model for you too.

Just remember that the secret to success is love plus passion plus a need in the market.

LESSONS AND CONFESSIONS:
KATHY CAPRINO ON REINVENTING
YOUR LIFE

For 18 years, I worked hard to build a high-level corporate marketing career. Despite being outwardly "successful," I grew chronically ill and miserable. For years I wanted something dramatically different, but I couldn't figure out what or how to do it.

Then, in the days following 9/11, I was laid off in a brutal way, and I snapped. I decided I'd never allow myself to live that way again — utterly devalued, demoralized, and completely lost. So I reinvented myself. I earned a Master's degree in marriage and family therapy, received coaching training, and launched a career coaching practice.

As I started to raise my profile and give talks to women, I noticed something shocking: 9 out of 10 working women I spoke with were as miserable as I had been! I decided then that I wanted to be part of the solution to this underground epidemic.

My company, Ellia Communications, now offers premier career, executive and leadership coaching programs and resources dedicated to helping professionals achieve breakthrough to the success and fulfillment they long for. As a supremely fulfilled executive coach,

*author and speaker, my career is what I dreamed of,
with more passion, power and purpose than I ever
thought possible.*

— Kathy Caprino

Founder, Ellia Communications
and Author of *Breakdown Breakthrough*

WHAT'S KEEPING YOU FROM LIVING YOUR PASSION?

IT'S NOT EASY TO FOLLOW the passion/love path. If it were
easy, 77 percent of the workforce wouldn't be passionless
in their jobs. Apathy and fear creep into our thoughts every
chance they get.

Apathy is that lost feeling you have when you try to
identify with something you care nothing about. Apathy is
the polite nod you give to the teller as she rambles on about
her morning. It's that face worn by the disenchanted factory
worker or the office worker who counts down to the end of
the eight-hour workday. Apathy is a lost soul.

Apathy does not care what she has for lunch and wants
YOU to choose the movie to go see. Apathy is easily distracted
by entertainment, and seeks all kinds of vices to fill the void
created by lack of meaning and purpose.

Apathy is not depression. It is acceptance of a lifestyle
that barely meets your minimum needs. Apathy is autopilot.
It turns you into a passenger, being swept hurriedly down the
many-forked currents of life without a paddle.

Passion is your paddle. Passion is your ability to choose
your future. With passion, you may not be able to choose the

river you are in, but you can sure as hell avoid the waterfalls; apathy wonders if it will see you bash your head on the rocks, and then yawns!

Apathy is a mist that hides all the doors and keyholes from your sight. Apathy is often why people never begin to truly live and do what they love.

Then there's fear. Fear is powerful and you can motivate people with it — sort of. While it does cause people to act, it usually makes them choose the poorest of decisions, if only because they are choosing for the wrong reasons.

Fear is the reason why it is thrilling to skydive. Fear is why failing feels like shit. Fear can be painful, and we will do just about anything to avoid it.

What are *you* afraid of?

Are you afraid of failing? Entrepreneurs experience 3.2 failures before achieving success, and as Jay Abraham said, "many achieve success only after their largest failure!"

And so the story goes for me... The first company I started failed. What I feared most about failing was what other people would think and the judgment that would be placed on me. I didn't want to see the "I-told-you-so" looks.

After having to face what I feared most about failing and surviving the shame I felt, I got over it and realized an important lesson that became my mantra:

**YOU MAY NOT BE WHERE YOU *WANT* TO BE,
BUT YOU ARE ALWAYS WHERE YOU *NEED* TO BE.**

The mistakes I made with my first company taught me invaluable lessons that I brought to my current company, Imaginarius. Failing made me a better business owner the next time around.

Are you afraid of succeeding? As you get to be more successful, life can change. Many people don't like change even if it's a good thing in the long run. Leaving your comfort zone can be challenging, but all the magic happens outside your comfort zone. That's where your greatest achievements and most memorable moments are found.

LIVING ON PURPOSE

LIVING A PURPOSE-FILLED LIFE MEANS being in sync with your core values in everything you do. It's how you give your best to the world. If you value adventure, do something you have never done before. If you value peace and quiet, do not join a rock band. If you value family, take them with you as you work abroad or work from home. If you value freedom, do not sign a long-term contract. If you value spirituality, help people. If you value health, treat your body right.

Living on purpose is easier said than done. It takes integrity. Integrity is what makes us trustworthy and makes people comfortable and know what to expect from us.

Integrity builds solid foundations on which to build your dreams. Integrity is your friend. Learn it, love it, act it, do it.

The enemy of integrity is *intentions*. How often do we "mean to" or "try" to do something? Integrity eats "mean to" and "try" for lunch.

Integrity is something people will follow. It is a trait of all great leaders. Without at least some of it, you might as well just tattoo a brick wall design on your forehead right now.

Intentions are responsible for most hurt feelings. Intentions cannot absolve repeated failures to deliver. Intentions are the excuses we give to poor decisions and ignorant actions. Intentions are not your friends.

Living by your principles and core values does not mean you have a stick up your ass. It does not mean that you are a snooty know-it-all. Living by your principles means you can answer clearly, quickly and honestly when called to explain your actions. Living by your principles means you can make good decisions with ease. Most of the time, anyway... I won't deny that some decisions and situations are much more challenging than others.

Living becomes easy when we can visualize our path unfolding before us and feel our purpose. Our path reveals itself when the mist clears. The mist clears when we know what we want. We define what we want by describing our ideal relationships, locations, habits, physical attributes, material things, and favored activities.

What I'm trying to get at here is that your life, everyone's life, is a story — and it is up to you to choose what kind of story you want it to be.

LOOKING WITHIN

CAN YOU TELL what kind of story I am? If you guessed *adventure,* then you're right. I see obstacles as trolls that must be conquered, and constantly search for new doors and the keys to unlock them.

What kind of book are you? What kind of life do you want? What do you enjoy watching or reading? If anything were possible, what kind of story would you live in?

Discover your language so that you can communicate better with yourself and other people. Find your voice and be heard. Find your passion and you will finally have something to say! Do what you love and find similar people attracted to you by the droves!

I speak from experience. People are attracted to someone who knows what they want. Be one of those people and you will discover an endless supply of opportunities and the help you need to maximize them.

Unfortunately, many people start businesses because they see an opportunity to make money or be successful, without ever defining what they want or what success means to them. They operate under one repeating mantra, one belief that goes something like: "If I make lots of money, I won't have to worry about anything."

Money, however, will not make the worry go away, since it cannot remove the thinking that caused worry in the first place. That's why your mindset is so important. You have to look inwards and visualize what success looks like for you and NOT to put a dollar amount on it — at least not yet.

Think about it like this. If you are constantly worried about health and you suddenly become a millionaire, you could go get all your checkups and see all your doctors, but you would eventually hear the same thing you heard before the money came: For overall good health, eat better and exercise more.

Do you actually imagine you will stop having health problems at that point? Do you honestly think a person will start running several miles a day and eating mostly vegetables and whole grains if they get more money?

Would the money fundamentally change who they are?

Probably not. A person who has health worries is likely to still have health worries even after making a lot more money — because money does not automatically change your habits, what are usually what make you sick in the first place.

Let's look at something else. How about someone who can never pay the bills? Will more money help her? Maybe temporarily, but this problem usually comes from living above one's means. With more money, this person would probably start adding on more monthly expenses like new cars, bigger houses and more credit cards, until she was swimming in debt again.

Money only enhances who we already are. If we are unhappy, more money makes us more miserable. If we are already happy, it brings us more happiness and affords us the opportunity to do more of the things that bring us joy. Money will only bring you more of what you already have.

LESSONS AND CONFESSIONS:
GABRIELLE BERNSTEIN ON
RECONNECTING WITH HER ~ING

When I was 21 years old I started a public relations business in Manhattan. I ran this business for five years. Though I was good at my job, the work never served me.

At the same time, I started a non-profit called the Women's Entrepreneurial Network. I always felt much more connected to the W.E.N. work than I did to my PR business.

Working in nightlife publicity in Manhattan can really take a toll on you. Late nights, negative people and a constant chase for more success led me to burn out fast. I hit a big bottom at 25 years old.

I realized that I couldn't find happiness in my credentials, a boyfriend or social status. I had to turn inward. This began my journey towards reconnecting with my ~ing (inner guide).

I got sober, picked up a serious meditation practice and became a student of A Course in Miracles. *Deep down I knew that I was meant to go through this hardship so that I could recover and teach others to do the same.*

That has been my path ever since. Today I am a bestselling author, speaker, and the founder of HerFuture.com, a social networking site for women to find mentors and be mentors.

LESSON LEARNED: *True happiness is not "out there" but a presence of inspiration and love that we must reconnect with inside ourselves.*

— Gabrielle Bernstein

Bestselling Author of *Spirit Junkie: A Radical Road to Self-Love and Miracles* 🜄

MAP ITEM –
Fusing Your Passion with Purpose

If you want to take on the world, first you need to take on *your* world. That starts by connecting your passion and what you love doing to your purpose.

What does the *happy* you do all day? What do you really love and have an abundance of passion for? If you still haven't found the love of your life, consider these questions:

1. If you didn't have to work for a salary to pay the bills, what would you spend your time doing?

2. What books and magazines do you like to read, and what do you like to learn about?

3. If you knew no one would judge your decision, what would you choose to do?

4. Consider all the activities you regularly do in a week. Which activities bring you the most joy and which bring you the most stress?

5. If you knew you wouldn't fail, what's the one thing you would try?

Often, societal roles lead us to lose sight of the things that once brought us so much joy. We become doctors to make our parents happy, salesmen to drive fancy cars, and lawyers because that's what a stupid test said you ought to do to have a happy, successful life.

In reflection, we can decide to stop accepting what is not working for us and begin to live our own lives. We can confide in the people closest to us to remember our fondest moments. We can reconnect with our passions that have become lost in the hustle and bustle of our daily lives. We can remember to put ourselves first and truly let the rest follow.

When thinking about your ultimate passion and what it is you really want to do, step into your little-girl shoes and jump back to when there were no limits to what you could be.

Now that we've cleared the mist, let's begin creating your Master Action Plan (MAP)! Grab a pen or marker and complete this sentence in big, bold letters:

The work I need to be doing to follow my passion and honor my purpose is

....

Say that sentence out loud. Does it feel good to say? Are you already doing what you're passionate about? Are you "in like" or "in love?" If it's love, you're ready to move on. If you need more time to think about it, TAKE THE TIME.

The important thing to realize is that you cannot waste time living in someone else's dream, story, or book. Wake up to *your* life! Honor your unique purpose and walk down your own path to greatness.

CHAPTER 2

It's All About Them:

FINDING A NICHE
AND FILLING A NEED

THE ONLY WAY TO PROFIT FROM YOUR PASSION

DO YOU KNOW WHO GARY HALBERT IS? He was a top copywriter and marketer who was well-respected by his peers. One day when he was lecturing, he asked his students this: If you and I were both selling hamburgers and we were competing to see who could sell the most, what advantages would you most like to have so you could win?

Lowest price, best meat, busiest location, more staff, and selling wholesale were a few of the answers that people came up with — none of which was the answer Gary Halbert was looking for. He told his audience that they could have every one of those advantages and he would beat them in the competition with his *one* advantage: "...a starving crowd."

That's the not-so-secret secret that many people just don't "get." I'll admit it took me a while to learn this myself:

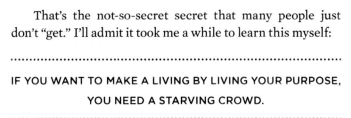

IF YOU WANT TO MAKE A LIVING BY LIVING YOUR PURPOSE, YOU NEED A STARVING CROWD.

Your starving crowd is your niche market, and it's the most important thing to get right when you build a business. Without it, you're stuck. You can't profit from your passion. You don't pass Go and you don't collect $200.

FINDING YOUR NICHE

SO WHAT IS A NICHE MARKET EXACTLY? A niche is a group of people with a common passion, interest, or pain who deeply want or need what you are offering. A niche has to be specific, but not so specific that there won't be enough customers to buy what you're offering.

For example, since we're talking about a starving crowd, let's say your passion is cooking. You dream of being the next Gordon Ramsey or Rachael Ray. "Cooking," "food," and "recipes" would all be way too broad in terms of a market. Consider these questions:

- What region do most of your recipes come from? Do you have a knack for Italian food, French cuisine, or Asian fusion?

- Who would use your recipes? Are your recipes quick, for busy women on the go? Are your recipes easy to follow, for people who aren't appearing on Iron Chef anytime soon?

- Do your recipes cater to people with certain dietary restrictions? Are you the queen of a gluten-free kitchen? Do you make vegan food that's to die for?

To get an idea of whether your niche is too broad –or too narrow — use the Google Adwords Keyword Tool to look at data for keywords that people in your niche would search for to find your business. Continuing with the food example, I might search for keywords like "gluten-free Italian recipes," "recipes children can make," and "vegan Asian dishes."

The Keyword Tool will tell you whether there is a high level of competition for your keywords. If that's the case, you should refine your niche further. It will also show the number of monthly searches for your particular keywords. If there are only a few hundred searches each month, the niche is likely too small to build a profitable business.

Now your niche should be more focused — for example, Italian food for vegans. With your unwavering passion and a starving crowd — literally — there will be no stopping you. You can set up a website and blog to your heart's content about your recipes, do your own weekly cooking show on YouTube and sell advertising slots, produce a cookbook, field questions and requests through social media, sell key ingredients paired with individual recipes (offer local delivery), offer your content through an app to expand your reach even further, take your products to trade shows, host your own cooking workshops...and that's just the beginning of **you** taking on the world!

Excited yet?

LESSONS AND CONFESSIONS:
Lea Woodward on Carving Out
a Niche and Creating
a Movement

Back in 2006, little did I know that my very comfortable life was about to change radically, nor that I was on the verge of creating a movement which would become something much bigger than I ever thought possible.

It all started with my husband being laid off from his job as an in-house designer. I was running a fledgling business as a holistic health coach, having escaped the corporate world a few months earlier, and we had all the trappings of a very comfortable lifestyle. And then it all changed.

We went into a panic — cutting back on our outgoings, trying to figure out what other jobs he could get — but we finally made a decision: we didn't want to be at anyone else's mercy any more. We were going to go it alone. And so we did.

But we went one step further and became location-independent — selling everything we owned to head off and run our business from a succession of lower-cost countries, just so we could live the lifestyle we wanted as our business grew without having to make so many compromises while the income was still unstable.

In the process, we carved a new niche and built an online community based around the concept of location independence.

The big idea we'd had for our business morphed into something we'd never even considered — earning a living helping others live a lifestyle of their choosing — and it's this premise which underpins our whole business today.

Were we scared things wouldn't work out? All the time. Did we have a grand plan all along that this is where we'd be and what we'd be doing? No.

LESSON LEARNED: *Nobody can tell you what's best for you. It's crucial that you make your own mistakes, learn what works for you and then follow your heart. It's only when you do this and follow your own path that you'll find the success you've been searching for.*

— Lea Woodward

Founder of Kinetiva

MAP ITEM –
DRAWING A PERSON IN YOUR NICHE

NEXT UP IN YOUR MAP I want you to focus on a person in your niche. Within the outline I want you to describe this person, your ideal customer. Who are they? Feel free to actually draw this out if you like doodling and want to get creative — or simply fill the outline with words describing the person.

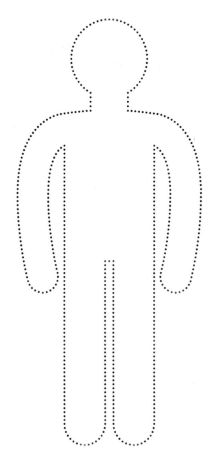

Consider the following:

- How old is this person?

- Is it a male or female?

- How does this person spend his or her free time?

- What kind of work does this person do?

- Is this person engaged or married?

- Does this person have children?

- How much money does this person earn?

As you move forward setting goals and building your brand and business, look back often at this person in your niche. Never lose sight of who your business serves, because without them you don't have a business.

PAIRING TRUST WITH NEED

THE BEST BUSINESS FOR YOU is one in which *you are part of your own niche.* That puts you in a power position of knowing your niche on an up-close-and-personal level. It also makes you more relatable to your potential customers and allows you to build trust faster.

My friend Tina is a cancer survivor. Her journey to recovery was hard-won. She now shares her inspiring story and helps other people who have been diagnosed with cancer. Her audience trusts her because she has been in the trenches — she's one of them. People want to work with people they can relate to and trust.

Being part of your own niche is a huge advantage, but you still have to do the research and discover what needs your niche has that you can fulfill with the products and services you're going to offer.

The best way to discover exactly what your niche needs is to ASK. Surveys are an effective way to do this. Every six months or so I use Survey Monkey 💧 to ask the *She Takes on the World* community what challenges they are facing, what I can do to help, and what their biggest needs are at that moment. My favorite question to ask and the one that prompts the most response is this: **"How can I help you?"**

These are some additional sample questions you can use to conduct your own survey:

- 💧 What is your current profession?

- 💧 What three blogs or websites do you most often visit within .... ?

- 💧 What concerns you most about .... ?

- 💧 If you could have one problem solved for you relating to .... , what would it be?

- 💧 How much money would you be willing to spend to have the above problem solved?

- 💧 What goal are you working towards?

- 💧 What one thing would help you achieve the above goal?

Share your survey on Facebook, Twitter, and your website, and email it to other people you know who fall within your niche. If you know people with relevant audiences, ask them to share it too. You want as many responses as you can get.

One of my most successful launches to date is the WE Mastermind program to help women entrepreneurs start online businesses. I partnered with Natalie Sisson, another phenomenal woman entrepreneur, and we spent nearly a year doing our research and making sure our program would feed a starving crowd.

We surveyed over 1000 women entrepreneurs in three separate surveys about a variety of challenges they were facing and what they needed help with. We carefully studied the results before creating a program, WE Mastermind, that confronted those needs and challenges head-on.

The result of this research and planning was a very successful launch, with hundreds of people tweeting and sharing the free video series we put out, thousands of women joining our tribe, and tens of thousands of dollars in sales — all in a matter of days.

Do the research. Give people what they are asking for. Feed a starving crowd.

CHAPTER 3

You Are What You Think:

SUPERCHARGE YOUR MIND

ARE YOU *READY* TO MOVE MOUNTAINS?

MY 25TH BIRTHDAY was the beginning of a new chapter in my life. It wasn't because I was a year older, nor did anything monumental happen to me.

It all started as I reviewed and worked on my MAP as I do every year around my birthday. I felt good about what I had accomplished and learned throughout the preceding year, but there were a couple areas of my business and my life that I felt were stagnant.

I climbed into a warm bath to meditate and reflect on how I could ignite all the pieces of my MAP for the upcoming year. As I pondered what I needed to do, my inner voice whispered that I just needed to be ready.

That was it!

Those areas of my life where I felt like I was up against a mountain, including getting this book written, were the areas where I was experiencing the most fear and holding onto doubt. What if I can't write a whole book and meet the deadlines? What if I do write a whole book and people don't love it? I had put the mountain in front of me.

It's easy to move a mountain once you can identify the thought patterns that put the mountain there in the first place. I closed my eyes and simply said, "I am ready. I am open to guidance and I am ready to achieve my greatness. I AM ready."

Being ready made the difference. Even though I had been working on being mindful of my thought patterns, and I have a daily meditation practice, I just wasn't *ready*. That one small shift in my thoughts moved my mountain, and a flood of inspiration, guidance, opportunities, and people came rushing in.

THE FOUNDATION OF A TAKING ON THE WORLD MINDSET

A "TAKING ON THE WORLD" MINDSET must be discovered, learned, executed and taught. I discovered it by accident, learned it by trial and error, and executed it by acting on my dreams. The foundation of the mindset is this:

....

**WORK NO MORE THAN ABSOLUTELY NECESSARY.
LIVE BY DISCOVERING WHO YOU TRULY ARE
AND LISTENING TO YOUR INNER VOICE.
AND LOVE YOUR LIFE BECAUSE YOU LOVE WHAT YOU DO
AND HOW YOU SPEND YOUR TIME.**

....

We've already talked about the importance of loving what you do if you're going to serve your true purpose and honor your authentic self. But let's talk about working no more than necessary — because many entrepreneurs seem to think working all the time is just part of the gig.

Work no more than absolutely necessary and you will be focused and dedicated. You will not spend time running in circles, chasing illusions or wasting time. Tim Ferris makes a strong case for exactly this in *The Four Hour Workweek* 🖊.

Maybe the "work" part for you is dealing with customers. If so, hire a manager and take slightly less money. Only deal with the biggest customer service issues, and empower your manager to fix the rest of the problems for you.

Maybe the "work" for you is bookkeeping and organizing receipts. Use Shoeboxed ⬗ to have your receipts scanned for you and turned into expense reports for as little as $99 per year. Hire a bookkeeper to stay on top of accounting tasks. The $60 per week you spend on this is worth the peace of mind. Only deal with paperwork when your bookkeeper can't handle the problem.

Decide what the "work" part of a business is for you and have a plan to hire some help. I'll be helping you with this later in the book. There is little point in suffering through something that someone else will gladly do for you in exchange for a bit of your profit. Save your energy for good decision-making and creative ideas to grow your business!

LESSONS AND CONFESSIONS:
TAMARA MINNS ON FINDING YOUR INNER STRENGTH

Once I decided I was ready to make the dream of owning my own business a reality, I began to see a change in the behavior of those I surrounded myself with. I learned very quickly that while most people were genuinely excited yet concerned for my well-being, it was also a test of my own personal strength and belief in myself. I believe many were perhaps jealous (doesn't everyone want to own a business?) and subtly questioned my integrity, my abilities, and my knowledge.

Ultimately, I had to believe wholeheartedly in myself and my dream, no matter what others thought of it. I had to be prepared for closed doors and keep walking towards my vision, though some thought I should wait. But what was it I should wait for? I knew what I wanted.

There is an inner strength found in becoming an entrepreneur that flourishes because of and in spite of the challenges and the naysayers. The strength of a woman is tested on a daily basis, especially one in a leadership role. There will always be someone threatened by my dream and success, but I have the confidence to know that if I dream big, good things will continue to come to me!

LESSON LEARNED: *Keep your mind focused on your dream, follow your gut, and keep those who truly believe in you close by for encouraging reminders that one doesn't need everyone's approval to move forward.*

— Tamara Minns

Founder of RareFunk.ca

MOVING PAST FEAR

WHATEVER IS HOLDING YOU BACK from the work you really want to be doing, it's time to move past the fear and move into action. And I'm talking NOW.

The rest of this book will be about creating your MAP and making things happen. Making things happen is the hard part, the part where people fail, the part where people leave their ideas as mere thoughts. It's time to let go of whatever is holding you back before we move forward.

When I was getting ready to leap into Imaginarius with my business partner, I had many fear-based thoughts go through my mind. I feared our personal relationship would be affected by being in business together. I worried that I was making a mistake going into another partnership, since the last partnership had failed. I was afraid of failing again and people questioning why I don't get a "real" job. I feared that my business partner wasn't as committed to the business as I was.

We all experience fear, especially when starting something new, but if we identify our fears and confront them head-on, we take away fear's power to control us and prevent us from living out our purpose.

I have a little ritual I do as part of my meditation practice when I need to release fear-based thoughts. I take out a piece of paper and cut it into pieces. On each piece, I write down a fear. If it pops into my head I write it down — no filtering. Then I burn each piece of paper one by one, letting my fears leave my mind and go up in smoke.

LESSONS AND CONFESSIONS:
LAUREN FRIESE ON OVERCOMING HER BIGGEST FEAR

Rejection comes fast and often when you're starting out, and when I started working on TalentEgg, my biggest fear was rejection.

Hustling to close TalentEgg's first-ever sale, I visited many offices and had many promising conversations. None was more promising than one with a leading telecom provider in Canada. They told me that they were "in," that they loved the product, and that they would have a contract to me in two weeks.

I marked it down as SOLD and called back two weeks later to collect the contract. Only their tune had changed. They didn't like the product after all, and they were no longer "in."

I sat and cried.

Within a few hours, I accepted it, I collected myself, and I got back to hustling. Three years later, I've been told "no" many (many) more times than I can count, but I now recognize that it's just part of business.

Lesson Learned: *Don't be afraid of hearing "no." It's an integral part of the process of running and growing a business.*

— Lauren Friese

Founder and CEO, TalentEgg.ca Inc.

MANTRAS AND MEDITATION TO SUPERCHARGE YOUR MIND

On my journey through Asia during my sophomore year of college, after that summer of working at the car factory, we visited quite a few temples where I would see monks sitting in meditation. It fascinated me that their lives were so simple and completely devoid of material things. They seemed to radiate pure happiness, so much so that it made ME happy just being in the presence of these meditating monks.

So one day I decided to give it a shot. I got down on the floor, eyes closed, palms up. I think the first thing I thought was, "What do the monks think about?"

Then I reflected on how grateful I was for the experience to be there. After one minute my wandering mind and impatience got the best of me. But it felt good to tune out the world and tune in to myself even for a minute. Soon I was committing to five minutes, then 10 minutes, then 20, then 30. I just felt so alive and connected to everything around me. It almost felt like I had a super power!

I started doing more yoga and reading Thich Nhat Hanh, Marianne Williamson, and *A Course in Miracles*. I became what Gabrielle Bernstein calls a "Spirit Junkie." Today, this is a daily practice involving meditation, mantras, and yoga that helped lead me to working happy and living on purpose.

I often get asked about my mantras. I have them on sticky notes on my night table, the computer in my office, and in other random places where I'll be reminded to take a second to breathe and refocus my mind. These are some of my mantras that you can use too:

→ I am attracting an abundance of prosperity and opportunity to my business

→ I am always led to my ideal clients who need what my business is offering

→ I am connecting with people who can help me live my purpose

→ Today I am one step closer to achieving

→ I am becoming wealthier every day that I follow my passion and honor my purpose

→ The fuel I put into my body is the fuel I get out of my body

→ What I give I get back in abundance

→ I alone am whole and have everything I need to take on the world

The key to developing your own daily practice is consistency. It takes 30 days to get into a new habit or routine, so figure out what works best for you and commit to being consistent. Do this for 30 days in a row and you will truly be unstoppable.

CHAPTER 4

The Inside-Out Business:

CREATING A BRAND AS A REFLECTION OF YOU

BUSINESS FROM THE INSIDE OUT

WHILE BORROWING INSPIRATION from someone else's dream is a great stepping stone, it cannot carry you through the entire process. I've tried it, and I can tell you it doesn't end well. I've learned this:

YOU ARE YOUR BUSINESS.

Early on, you must find a way to make your creation your own, personal to you. Someone else's idea of beauty, perfection or cause is nice, but it is not your own. It cannot ever push you to work as hard as will a creation that you feel is a whole reflection of you.

Connect with your inner desires and let them be a large reflection of who you are and what you create on the outside. It will make all the difference.

WHAT KIND OF BUSINESS OWNER ARE YOU?

NOW THAT YOU HAVE POURED the mold for your business foundation, you might want to consider what type of business owner you are. To find this out, you need to consider your personality and how you feel comfortable running things.

An entrepreneurial spirit will usually walk down one of two business roads:

1. As a sole proprietor or in a partnership, you build a small business that allows you the freedom to work from home, take care of your children, travel, or whatever else you want to do. You are content with being a small business owner and aren't looking to build the next Google. (Today, though, you can be a small business and have still a globally recognized brand, thanks to the power of the Internet!)

2. You want to build what I like to call a legacy business, one that will hopefully stand the test of time. Think Coca-Cola, Hearst Corporation, *Forbes*. You want to be a major power player, and the thought of one day becoming a publicly-traded company excites you.

Smaller or local business owners are usually in competition for a relatively small share of the market. These people thrill at the newness and challenge of creating a business, but soon tire of the dream once the business becomes established and operations become routine. They are often too creative to make efficient managers, and drive their team crazy with new ideas and tasks. Start-up teams in this environment are often mystified as to what new idea gets priority and what exactly the boss has in mind.

It is also often hard for a creative spirit to survive the monotonous climb to becoming a Fortune 500. Most often, this type would be much happier just running the maze of activities that comes with start-up territory, then selling it or moving on to something new.

The more rare breed of entrepreneur has the patience, stamina and vision to grow a large company. These people get that slow and steady wins the race. They are calculated and methodical, adhering closely to their visions and goals. They often bend rules and take an unconventional approach to attaining their goals; this is a form of creativity, but even more so an indicator of leadership.

These people put their teams at ease with daily and weekly routines and tasks. They understand priorities and what's important, don't respond willy-nilly to every little distraction, and are excellent communicators. These are people with a plan, and they follow the plan and expect those around them to do so as well.

Once you have decided which environment suits you best, you can then determine the types of roles and presence you would like to have in your company. Defining your role or roles is an essential part of your success.

Some people prefer to work alone, meeting only with their teams as a necessity or for maintenance, while others thrive on being surrounded by personalities that add spice to their lives and act as feedback machines.

Some people love the idea of online-only sales, outsourcing all their managers and employees, while others are more inventive and may choose to become salesmen for their patented ideas.

It is not vital to choose at this stage, but I did want to assure you that there is a model that can work for *you!*

LESSONS AND CONFESSIONS:
ADRIENNE GRAHAM ON PUTTING YOURSELF FIRST

What started as a small networking group evolved into an international power brand. But it wasn't without bumps, bruises and hard lessons learned.

Over the years the purpose of Empower Me has changed. The vision and mission is to empower people to live their best professional (and entrepreneurial) lives. I had lofty goals for the company. A quarterly magazine, radio station, Internet TV channel, a learning institute, coaching and products to help people achieve their professional goals — just to name a few.

I bootstrapped the business along with help from "friends" who offered to help for nothing in return. They believed in me and the mission.

Somehow, their passion waned as the economy failed around us. Suddenly I was told I couldn't make it work, I couldn't make it happen and that I should give up.

Call it stubbornness or ingrained passion, but I chose to cut off the negative people, shut down the business temporarily (I was experiencing some painful events so I needed a break), and started healing and rebuilding.

Empower Me has made an amazing recovery and we're in launch mode on several products. The brand has exploded (in a great way). Backers and clients are more supportive than ever and have appreciated my transparency in sharing with them. Client activity has picked up and Empower Me is back to helping people live their best professional lives.

So to those who said I couldn't, guess what? I CAN! And I did.

Lesson Learned: *Not everyone has your best interests at heart. You can be your own enemy if you fall victim to the negativity.*

— Adrienne Graham

Founder & President,
Empower Me! Corporation

SUCCESS IS IN YOUR STORY

Fond of observing people and cultures, I found myself sitting in a large square in Cusco, Peru, enjoying the sights and sounds of the many people gathered there. I happened to notice a young woman taking a very different approach to her business than the many merchants around her.

There is much poverty in Peru, and wherever there are flocks of bag-addled tourists, there are simple crafters pushing their souvenirs. Even in a mob of hungry sellers, all offering similar-looking woven necklaces and bracelets, this woman managed to stand out from the crowd. Her method was soft and simple, but potent and captivating in its effect.

A normal conversation in the oversaturated market square would typically go something like this:

"You buy beautiful necklace or bracelet?"

"No, thank you."

"But it's very beautiful and I give you a good price."

"No, thank you."

The tourist would turn a disinterested head in search of something less banal.

A conversation with this clever young lady tended to sound more like this:

"Hello, my name is Maria. What is your name?"

"Oh, hi. I'm Ellen."

"Hi Ellen. Nice to meet you. Where are you visiting my country from?"

"The United States."

"Oh, I see, and what do you hope to see in my beautiful country?"

"I came to see Machu Picchu and experience the Peruvian culture."

"Ah yes. A sacred site and very beautiful mountains."

After a minute or so of polite banter she would pull a half-woven necklace from her bag and begin to explain how she makes each piece by hand using the finest alpaca wool and natural dyes. She would then emphasize how long it takes her to make a quality piece and how she is passionate about her work because she's making something that honors the traditions of her country.

She wasn't just asking people for a sale; she was telling a well-crafted story. Maria understood that she *is* her business.

Her pieces were no more beautiful than the rest, her materials came from the same place, and she took no longer than anyone else to make each piece.

The truth Maria had discovered and what she reminded me that day is this:

**PEOPLE BUY INTO A PERSON, A STORY,
AN IDEA — NOT MERELY A TRINKET.**

By appreciating the importance of conversation, she was creating what the tourist had actually come to Peru to find: an authentic experience. The bauble was merely a representation of that exchange, and came with a nice story for the tourists to take back home to friends and family.

A story is better than any mission statement you could craft for your brand. Your story is social currency. What do I mean by that? I mean that people like to talk, and if you give them something entertaining to talk about, they will unconsciously perceive it as valuable. That's currency. Give your customers that currency, and they will buy from you over and over again.

If you can be wise like Maria and find what your customers are truly after, you will have everything you need. Don't reinvent the wheel. When articles, books and people stress the importance of differentiating your product, just think of Maria's story and know that the truth about sales lies not in the product but in the salesman. You want a competitive edge? Learn to tell a great story.

MAP ITEM –
WRITING YOUR STORY

EVERYONE HAS A STORY. It's time to tell yours and let your business and brand grow around it. It is best to keep it short and sweet. Aim to write your story in the space provided. Consider some of these questions, if you're stuck:

- ⊛ Who are you and what need do you fulfill?

- ⊛ What makes you unique?

- ⊛ What is your passion and how did you find it?

- ⊛ How are your products or services produced?

- ⊛ Why do you understand your customer better than the competition?

....

....

....

....

....

....

....

....

....

....

....

....

....

....

....

....

....

....

....

....

....

....

....

....

....

....

To take it one step further, we're going to transform a story into a powerful visualization tool.

Look into the future at what you want for yourself when you reach your goals. Write your story again, *but* write it from where you'll be in ten years. Keep it in present tense. Read it often when you review your MAP.

This is a powerful visualization tool that *She Takes on the World* contributor Debra Eckerling helped me discover. I love it because it reminds me of Napoleon Hill's teachings from my favorite book, *Think and Grow Rich* 🔹, a must read for anyone with an entrepreneurial spirit.

CHAPTER 5

The Bigger Picture:

A Bold Plan for a New Breed of Entrepreneurs

SMALL STEPS TOWARDS BIG GOALS

ANYTHING BIG YOU'RE GOING TO ACCOMPLISH is not going to be accomplished overnight, next week or next month. Big goals require perseverance and stamina. Every day, you need to be active in moving forward towards your goals — and that can become exhausting, trust me.

That's why the main component of the MAP is a Bigger Picture Strategy (BPS) and that's the next part of your MAP we're going to focus on. It keeps your eye on the prize when the going gets tough!

Each morning I look at my BPS so I can see what I need to do to meet my next milestone. I repeat the mantra, "Today I get five steps closer to reaching my goal," and I commit to completing five tasks for the day.

Now, if you're like me, you aren't just working on *one* idea, product, or brand — and that's not a bad thing. If you're one of those women who is a multitasker and can't have it any other way, I'm not going to be the one to tell you that you need to learn to focus on one thing.

What makes multitasking unproductive is when you jump into one thing after another without COMPLETING anything. If you're quitting halfway through each race you start, you will never get the satisfaction of completing a goal, and you will quickly lose momentum. Losing momentum spells a slow and painful death for any business.

Besides being painful, people around you will sense the weakness in your resolve and begin to inject their own ideas, desires, and fears into your business. People are just like that. They honestly don't mean any harm, but it can spell the end for you.

BALANCING BASKETS

FOR THOSE OF YOU who don't want to put all your eggs in one basket (like me!) you have to learn to structure your day a little differently, keeping your integrity in check and your baskets somewhat balanced.

For example, in any given day I am working on Imaginarius and projects for our clients, *She Takes on the World,* and WE Mastermind. I am also writing articles for various media outlets, and building and pushing my personal brand.

In my office I have a white board that is split into "baskets" that are labeled with each of my major projects and initiatives. I write out each of my daily tasks on sticky notes. As I complete tasks, I put the sticky notes in the appropriate baskets on my white board.

Throughout the week, this paints a clear picture of what I've spent my time on. And for a visual person like myself, I must admit that I have a ton of fun doing this!

Some weeks things look pretty balanced. Other weeks the white board looks pretty chaotic, and that's okay too. We women can drive ourselves insane trying to keep everything balanced. I want you to let go of trying to attain this fantasy equilibrium in your life. Work-life balance just doesn't exist. More about that later.

LESSONS AND CONFESSIONS:
NICOLE WILLIAMS ON
PERSEVERANCE

One of the defining moments in my career so far was when my agent called to say Penguin Group was offering me a book deal. I was in the car on my phone, and I had to pull over to absorb it. I had worked so long and hard for it to come to fruition.

It was unthinkable that I was going to be a published author. To sell the book in New York City, when so many people had doubted me, was amazing. It was affirmation that I was going to succeed and I knew it would be a major accomplishment in my life.

I realized it's not the people most talented who succeed. It's the ones who play the game the longest.

LESSON LEARNED: *Beyond skill, talent, charisma, beyond all attributes... success comes from perseverance and the ability to not give up when everything points toward failure. You have to continue on course towards your vision, and it may take longer than you ever thought possible. So enjoy the ride.*

— Nicole Williams

Founder of WORKS by Nicole Williams
and Bestselling Author of *Girl on Top*

BIGGER PICTURE PLANNING

LET'S GO BACK to the Bigger Picture Strategy. My BPS has pretty much taken the place of a business plan for me now, and I attribute most of my success to following it.

The BPS is an annual activity for me where I combine goal setting, strategic planning, and vision boarding. I usually do it around my birthday, preferably in a place with no distractions.

It starts with drawing out five big goals based on your ideal future and active passions. These goals are most effective when they *aren't* easily accomplished. Stretch your brain to the outer limits of your rational thinking and imagination. Imagine your ultimate success.

Got it? Now, what do you see next? That's the bigger picture mindset; what happens *after* you have attained what you say is already possible?

Once I have my five big goals, I write strategic actions and set milestones for each goal. These can be marketing actions, reaching out to people, and so on. Here is an example of one goal and strategic actions to go with it:

- 🌍 **GOAL:** Land a writing gig for a *major* magazine or online publication

- 🌍 **STRATEGIC ACTIONS:**

  - From January to June, publish two blog posts each week

  - Contact five blogs with a large readership and pitch relevant guest posts

  - Build Facebook fan page to 1,000 fans to show the magazine there is an existing readership and fan base

- Prepare pitch, including recent blog posts, guest posts, and other writing samples

- Research the names and contact information for editors at major publications and send customized pitch

From here, formulate a checklist to stay on track. I let my strategic actions determine my day-to-day schedule and activities.

The funny thing about developing an original system is that it feels like brand-new territory when you are creating it. However, when I read back over my own words and advice, I can see the same tones and themes emerge from my process as those of other entrepreneurs I admire and who have been able to accomplish incredible things.

That's an exciting part for me and one thing I get from explaining my methods. I get to see the truth revealed as I search for the best words to communicate effectively to you. And those same words echo back from other driven entrepreneurs:

DREAM, CARE, PLAN, ACT, CHECK, REDEFINE, BALANCE, CREATE, LEARN, ADAPT, LOVE, AND LIVE.

The entire process seems less like work when it's you who has decided that a step is necessary. How you come to that decision is your learning curve.

What I mean is that all these processes may sound overwhelming right now, but when you begin them with your end goal in mind, the steps required to reach the goal will crystallize faster than you might expect. What's needed often becomes obvious very quickly, and you will be choosing those steps yourself.

One choice that is mine in tailoring this process is to use the number five. It's my magic number: five goals, five milestones and five daily tasks. Every day I try to do five things that will push me forward in reaching my five big-picture goals.

There is no rational explanation behind my obsession with the number five for strategic planning and goal setting. I take it simply as one happy variable I can control, and it works for me. Not too overwhelming, but not comfortable either. For me, comfort means I'm not pushing myself to learn and that can get in the way of real progress. Just like the flame of hunger, discomfort is a powerful motivator.

So what comes after all my fives? Vision boarding! If you're into scrapbooking you can get really creative and have a lot of fun here. I incorporate mini vision boards into my BPS because you have to picture what your life will look like after achieving a goal. It's not enough to just picture it, though; you also have to look at it every day and *feel* it.

I like vision boarding the classic way — by collecting images from magazines and photos that inspire me. I realize there are apps for this now, but I personally feel that it's not the same. There is quite a process to choosing just the right visuals to express your desires. I never settle for "good enough" when I do a vision board, and if I can't find a visual, I create it.

Don't underestimate the power of having your dreams accessible in a visible, tangible form. In the space between an idea's birth and its full physical fruition are all the steps, actions and visualizations that can get you there.

So, that is my process: a glimpse into my head, heart and soul; the boiled-down recipe to my success.

Recipe to Success

INGREDIENTS:

- ✓ 2 cups of passion
- ✓ 1 cup of blood, sweat and tears
- ✓ 1 enormous dream
- ✓ 5 huge goals with deadlines
- ✓ 5 big milestones with deadlines
- ✓ 5 balancing baskets
- ✓ 1 checklist
- ✓ 1 vision board
- ✓ Dash of courage
- ✓ Pinch of inspiration
- ✓ Generous dollop of love

Preheat oven to awesome.

Mix all dry ingredients in a large bowl. Carefully sift the mixture, removing any bullshit you see. When mixture appears smooth and honest, add blood, sweat and tears. Mix vigorously, as if your life depended on it, and place in a covered pan on a warm stove. Wait for the potential to rise. Once you're afraid it will topple over, throw it into the oven and bake until golden brown. Repeat.

Serves a lifetime.

MAP ITEM –
Your Bigger Picture Strategy

THIS IS A KEY COMPONENT of your MAP, so spend some time on this section. Get creative with it, since you're going to be looking at it a whole lot in the future. The only rule is for at least one of your goals to be financially-related — for example, an income projection or a product launch with a revenue goal attached to it. Your financial goal will likely be linked to or dependent on some of the other goals in the BPS. It is important to have at least one financial goal so that you can live your passion *and* make a living.

- ꙮ This MAP section combines goal setting with vision boarding so you'll want to use a blank notebook, or poster paper.

- ꙮ Write down the first goal, followed by five strategic actions or milestones you'll need to complete to accomplish the goal.

- ꙮ On the same page or on a separate page if you prefer, glue or tape images from magazines and photographs that help you visualize reaching the goal and what your life will look like with that goal accomplished.

Repeat the last two steps for each goal you set. Then look lovingly and often upon the Bigger Picture Strategy you've created for yourself.

WHAT ABOUT A BUSINESS PLAN?

Some of you may be thinking, "Okay, Natalie, the BPS is awesome and all, but don't I need a formal business plan too?"

In my last business class of college, I had to write a huge formal business plan with a group. It was beautifully put together and packed with bullshit.

I always found the process of writing formal business plans to be a waste of my time. Not that planning isn't important; I just think there's a more practical (and enjoyable!) way *if* you don't need investors or a loan to make your business dream a reality.

When launching a new business or product, I like to create a Compass (the Compass). It's short and sweet and helps you consider some important questions that you should be able to answer.

MAP ITEM –
Your BUSINESS COMPASS

WANT TO CREATE YOUR OWN COMPASS? Answer each of the following ten questions. Keep your answers short and sweet. You should not need more than the few lines provided to write your answers. Even though the Compass is short, there is a considerable amount of thought that goes into it. Many of the answers will likely become clear in upcoming chapters of the book. Also, consider this to be a work in progress! Reflect on your plan and refine when necessary.

1. What is your vision for your business?

....

....

....

....

2. Who is going to buy your product or service? (Age, gender, location, education level, income, marital status, hobbies, etc.)

....

....

....

....

3. What need — or desire — are you going to fulfill within your niche market?

....

....

....

....

4. Who are your top three competitors? What makes you stand out?

1. ....

2. ....

3. ....

5. What expenses will you incur as you start and run your business? As a general rule, you should be able to cover your expenses for at least three months while you find your first customers.

ITEM	COST

6. What is your personal income goal, based on the amount of money required to live your ideal lifestyle? (Housing, transportation, entertainment, travel, etc.)

....

7. What is the sale price of your product or service? How many items will you have to sell to cover your expenses *and* meet your personal income goal? After calculating how many products you have to sell to reach your goal, re-examine your price point and consider adjusting it. In my experience, it is easier and less time-consuming to sell fewer units at a higher price point than to sell more units at a low price point. Many women entrepreneurs under-value the products and services they produce and sell. Don't make that mistake. You need to earn what you're worth to take on the world!

$$\frac{Expenses + Personal\ Income\ Goal}{Sale\ Price\ Per\ Item} = \begin{array}{c} Number\ of\ Items \\ You\ Have\ to\ Sell \end{array}$$

8. How are you going to distribute your product or service?

....

....

....

....

9. How are you going to market your product or service? I recommend coming back to this question after reading Chapter Nine.

....

....

....

....

10. Who's going to be on your team, and what will each person's role be? Consider partners, employees, contractors, mentors, etc. I recommend coming back to this question after reading Chapter Seven.

....

....

....

....

You will likely need time to think about these questions, so feel free to come back to your Compass when you're ready. Remember that the most important part of planning is that you do what works for you!

CHAPTER 6

Women Entrepreneurs as Change Agents:

THE BUSINESS OF CHANGING THE WORLD

IT REALLY IS A SMALL WORLD AFTER ALL

If you haven't already learned this about me, I want to change the world. Yes, a bold undertaking, I know. But thanks to the Internet, we have an opportunity to create a bigger impact than ever before, and at *very little cost.*

For the price of a small video camera and some software, we can promote mini-films on YouTube. With an investment of time, we can tweet and provide Facebook content to the hungry masses or important few.

And through crowdfunding platforms like Kickstarter ◊ we can spread ideas and raise funds for a project.

The learning curve is small, and the rewards are great.

Caring about your work is not to be underestimated. I care that my work has meaning and makes an impact. I care about this far more than I care how much money I make, and that passion and honesty creates the real momentum behind the projects I bring to life.

Having a good salary is a perk, but it doesn't fulfill me the way I feel fulfilled when someone tells me how the work I did has made a difference in their life.

A great example comes from an experience I had while working on *Out My Window,* the interactive documentary that my company Imaginarius developed with the National

Film Board (NFB), and for which my business partner and I won an EMMY®.[i]

I was at an airport in South America and I found myself trying to explain to someone exactly what I do (which, by the way, sounded strikingly similar to my list of "all the things I want to be when I grow up").

As I began to tell the story of how we developed this interactive documentary about life in high-rise buildings around the world, a woman standing in front of me spun around and asked, "Are you talking about *Out My Window?*"

I was shocked. "Yes! My company designed and built the interactive architecture!" Excitedly, she went on to explain that the project really touched her, and for the last three weeks she had been showing it to several people and had intended to get in touch with the company that did the development.

Goosebumps crept up my arms. Here I was, thousands of miles from home, and someone knew my work and was impacted by it. Wow. That impact is what I live for.

MAKING MEANING

While traveling, I have met people who follow me on Twitter, read *She Takes on the World,* or have read articles I've written for other media outlets. Putting content out there online, whether it's a blog, a website, or a video, enables us to measure our reach to people around the world. When we can put faces to the numbers, it suddenly takes on a whole new meaning!

I have a habit of asking women entrepreneurs why they went into business. I hear myself do this with women I meet

---

i   EMMY® is a registered trademark of the National Academy of Television Arts & Sciences at events, conferences, speaking engagements, you name it. What I'm happy to report I'm learning is that an increasing number of women are more concerned about making meaning than making money.

I have no doubt in my mind that women entrepreneurs *are* changing the world, and if we can recruit more women to commit to doing meaningful work they are passionate about, imagine the impact we will have.

LESSONS AND CONFESSIONS:
ANA ALEXANDRA ON POURING PROFITS INTO POSITIVE SOCIAL IMPACT

Nicaragua's history has produced strong, persistent, loving, and hardworking people with big dreams and a unique perspective on life. I am such a woman.

I had a very successful career, but my dream was to develop my own product line that I would personally design. I founded KUERO as a sole proprietorship in 2005 with the purpose of creating designer handbags in Nicaragua, each individually handcrafted with the finest leather available in our country.

Within six months I had 90 unique handbags, which became my first leather handbag collection.

With hard work, persistence, and commitment to my country, KUERO is today the first Nicaraguan brand of its kind to expand to an international market. I am now using my success to make a positive social impact in my country.

My vision is to create a technical training school for young adults that creates a new workforce of skilled, qualified artisans in Nicaragua. We have enacted a Social Responsibility Program to invest in young adults, providing them with the opportunity to finish high school and have access to a college education. I know there is so much more to come.

LESSON LEARNED: *True success lies not just in discovering and following your own purpose, but in giving others the opportunity to find their purpose too.*

— Ana Alexandra Velazquez Castro

Founder of KUERO

SOCIAL ENTREPRENEURS RISING

IN 2003, JENNY BUCCOS decided she wanted to turn her love of travel and world cultures into a social enterprise. After months of brainstorming, Jenny founded ProjectExplorer.org with the plan to educate young people by presenting compelling stories of the world's cultures, histories, and peoples. Now, nearly two million students and educators around the world have experienced the videos and lessons produced by Jenny and her team.

Jenny represents a growing number of social entrepreneurs brimming with enthusiasm and ready to change the world. Jenny has this advice for women wanting to start a not-for-profit organization or social enterprise:

Spend time building your business. I see so many people who want to jump right in with the programming part of their businesses and nonprofits. It's understandable; it's the sexy part of what they want to do. By getting everything in order — a clear mission statement, market research, your Board of Directors and team, collateral materials, etc. — you have set yourself up for success when you eventually launch your business.

I know from experience that if you want to change the world with your not-for-profit organization, you have to treat it like a business from day one. So if it's meaning you want to make, apply the business lessons in this book and there will be no stopping you.

LESSONS AND CONFESSIONS:
REHMAH KASULE ON ESTABLISHING AN INTERNATIONAL ORGANIZATION

In 1998, two years after university, I quit my job as a graphic designer and I started my own agency in Uganda with no funding, no experience, and no guidance. With commitment, endurance and focus, the agency has grown its portfolio to include powerful local and international brands. It is this experience that gave me the desire to start Century Entrepreneurship Development Agency, known as CEDA International, in 2007. I wanted to nurture young women in Uganda and beyond to embrace entrepreneurship as a career option so that they become job creators, not job seekers.

With the vision of creating a new generation of women leaders who are economically independent and socially responsible, the organization mentors women to discover their lives' purposes, and develop key leadership and entrepreneurship skills.

We have supported over 16,700 youth, women, and people living with HIV/AIDS to improve their livelihoods in Uganda, Tanzania, and Rwanda. Our Mentoring Walks have connected more than 775 girls and women for mentoring partnerships. The Rising Stars Mentoring Program won the U.S. State Department Innovation Award 2010, and is impacting more than 12,000 girls in secondary schools and universities. Our work in empowering women was recognized at the Presidential Summit on Entrepreneurship hosted by President Barack Obama in Washington, DC.

LESSON LEARNED: *Empowering women can change the world; if we mentor women, we take care of everyone.*

— Owek. Hajat Rehmah Kasule

Founder of CEDA International and Author
of *From Gomba to the White House:
The Journey of an African Woman Entrepreneur*

LEAVING A LEGACY

WHEN I FLY I always make sure to book a window seat well in advance. I love looking down on the world from up in the air because it puts everything into perspective for me. It makes me feel that we are all interconnected.

Our actions and the energy we create, positive or negative, matters. It matters to the people around us with whom we have direct contact, and it also matters to people we haven't even met. No one is too insignificant to make a difference. We can all leave a lasting legacy that transforms the world in some way.

As part of the *She Takes on the World* brand, I want to inspire and support women entrepreneurs globally, including those in developing countries. I want entrepreneurial women around the world to have the chance to start businesses and lift their families from poverty.

That's why I love Kiva.org 🜄, a microlending platform that allows anyone to loan as little as $25 to an entrepreneur in a developing country. You choose who you want to lend to (I focus on women), and once your loan is paid back by the entrepreneur you can loan it again and again and again. So your $25 can transform many lives as you give entrepreneurs the opportunity to create their own jobs and provide for their families. If this sounds like something you'd like to be involved in, head to kiva.org/teams/shetakesontheworld. Join the *She Takes on the World* lending team and connect with fellow women entrepreneurs who are making loans to change the lives of women entrepreneurs globally. It's a beautiful thing!

Empowering entrepreneurs is just one way you can give back and leave a legacy. If you're interested in supporting girl's education, an organization I love is She's the First 🜄, which gives girls in developing countries the opportunity to attend school. If you're appalled by the fact that 1000 girls and women die each day during pregnancy and childbirth, become part of the solution with the White Ribbon Alliance 🝆.

Don't be overwhelmed by the number of people, causes, and organizations that could benefit from your help. Instead, focus on giving back in a way that *feels* right for you. Ask yourself this question that I often ask myself:

HOW CAN I USE MY PASSION AND EXPERTISE TO MAKE THE WORLD A BETTER PLACE?

No matter what you want your legacy to be, just know that we can all make a difference.

CHAPTER 7

Everyone Needs a Team:

How to Build One When You're on a Budget

YOU JUST CAN'T DO IT ALL

SOME PEOPLE DO LOVE TO FLY SOLO, and those entrepreneurial spirits who reject the constraints of working with others may lose more from making that decision than they might imagine.

Spending a few seconds looking up the "Oprahs" and "Martha Stewarts" of the world will reveal vast networks of contacts and highly-structured, if not specialized, teams. Both of these women would be quick to admit that teams are their lifeblood and they would be nowhere without them.

A solo entrepreneur is a bit like a tightrope walker. While it's impressive to walk a tightrope without a net, all those "ohhs" and "ahhhs" will quickly turn into bitter "I tried to tell hers" and head-shaking when the inevitable fall comes. Basically, you will win the admiration of those around you, only to lose it quickly when you encounter roadblocks along the way.

No one person can do everything and, in my opinion, it's just unwise and egotistical to think that you can.

There is a widespread misconception that working from home or working virtually means that you are working alone. I blame this prevailing myth for all the solo acts that read a book and jump eagerly into the water, only to turn belly up under their first big wave.

Unless you are looking to tan your tummy, believe me when I say that every owner I have talked to thinks of her team as the foundation of her success. I like to think of it as taking a gorgeous pair of Manolo Blahniks and sawing off the heel. *Ouch!* Why, god, why, right? Exactly. Every smart woman with vision has a Manolo Blahnik inside her. It's the solo acts that cut themselves short at the heel!

Take a good look at yourself right now. Are you *that* woman entrepreneur? Are you doing the admin work, book-keeping, sales, marketing, distribution, and every other task under the sun all by yourself?

Is it because you feel like you're not making enough money to justify hiring help? If so, worry not. The whole hiring help vs. can't afford it argument is a Catch-22 many entrepreneurs face. In my experience, you can't afford *not* to hire help.

I'm going to say that again. You CAN'T AFFORD to oper-ate alone. You will free up more time for important tasks that will GENERATE REVENUE, as opposed to tedious tasks that don't bring in the dough. I've been there, and I know how much better business is on the other side.

ACT LIKE AN OWNER

THE CONCEPT OF HIRING help when you feel you aren't gen-erating enough revenue is a difficult concept to grasp, but it is essential to your future success. I sincerely don't want to see you work yourself to the bone and become burned out before the business has had a real chance to lift off the ground.

If you are going to micro-manage and do the repetitive tasks, you might as well go work for someone else, do *their* repetitive tasks, and take no risk for the losses they might incur. You are an owner and you need to act like one, so don't act like an employee.

Let me paint you a picture of what I mean.

Jill opened a cute specialty coffee shop in a small town. She is a beautiful mess of a person with more passion in her little pinky than most of us would dare imagine. Her "whatever it takes" attitude is matched only by her wild creativity, and she is normally a bubbling cauldron of ideas.

Normally is the key word here. Everything began with a bang. She decided on a vision, taken from her passion, expanded the idea, wrote a great business plan and took off with both feet running. Her summer was a maze of trial and error, but she finally settled into a routine that managed to keep the business afloat.

Fast forward to just one year later, however, and my friend Jill had become a ghostly vision of her former self. She no longer joked and bubbled, she had gained a considerable amount of weight, and wore new stress lines on a usually vibrant and unblemished face.

Cautiously, I approached her and asked how things had been going. "Fine," she offered with a defeated sigh. Fine? This woman was a lot of things, but "fine" had never been one of them.

"You look a bit tired," I observed, and watched her face closely for reaction. Her shoulders drooped and she let out another sigh. "Yeah, well, what can you do, you know? I'd love to take some time off to do some new promotions and maybe get a bit of sleep, but with all this paperwork and the cost of help these days, I just need to keep at it."

There it is, people. The attitude that turns so many bright souls into dull, gray, automatons — and it's *her* business! Did you hear the flawed thinking? Did you catch the "stuck" attitude?

Why had she gained weight? Why was she so tired? Why did she not do what she *wanted* to do?

Her common sense was correct. She needed a break and she needed to change up her promotions, but her reasoning told her a different story. I'll explain this in a bit.

She had gained weight because she had drowned herself in paperwork and daily operations that any bookkeeper could do for $40 per week and any employee could do for $10.00 per hour. While this seems like money she does not have, what her tired brain does not realize is that she needs to re-invest in her company.

Unfortunately, I know too many women like Jill. I've even been there myself.

Every business must grow, and how you handle these growing pains will determine your future as a business owner. People often forget to step back and look at how their business models are working under current conditions with current knowledge.

What do you think would have happened if Jill had taken the plunge and invested a bit more money into her business one month—hired a couple of employees to run her shop, and a bookkeeper? She would have paid out more, yes, but what would she have gained?

She would have gained TIME. With more time on her hands, she could have gotten some much-deserved rest. Then her tired mind would be fresh. Perhaps with a fresh mind she would decide to start a new campaign for her coffee shop that would drive more business.

With her driving in more business, sales would go up, covering the cost of her employees and additional expenses.

Time and rest are two invaluable things a leader needs to make any business a success. Work smart, my friends, not hard.

It is very easy to fall into Jill's trap — easier than you would think. We are predisposed to it. We are conditioned, brought up that way.

Jill was the person I would have thought to be in the *least* danger of losing sight of what was important, but when faced with mounting bills, paperwork and pressure, her reasoning became a powerful adversary to her progress.

Your reasoning will tell you that you need to be safe, keep doing what you're doing, and to resist change. It does this because you tire yourself out and fall prey to a routine. The tired mind hypnotizes itself and follows the same patterns that got stuck there in the first place.

YOUR TEAM IN THE CLOUD

Now, I'M NOT TELLING YOU that you need full-time employees who work alongside you. I talk to a lot of women who just want to run a business from home — or abroad — and don't necessarily *want* employees.

For a while I worked alongside a team of contractors in a small office, and I quickly learned that I don't want employees! They were brilliant and did amazing work, but keeping them motivated was exhausting. I quickly let their problems become my own and tried to take a motherly role to help them put the pieces of their lives together.

I find that I'm more productive working with a small virtual team right now because of the dreams I'm currently chasing and the amount of traveling I do.

What I really want to express is that it's okay if you don't want to build the next big global corporation. It's okay if you want to stay small and have time for other things in life, like raising a family or traveling the world, but you need help. We all do.

This is where a virtual team can come in handy. I really believe that we must adapt to the times or risk becoming victims of our own choices.

During the recession, we saw an uptick in freelance work, and many people started businesses out of necessity. Companies weren't, and still aren't, hiring like they used to. This is becoming the new norm, and will only become more prevalent as the years pass.

A virtual hire can help you do *anything*. These are just some of the tasks you might want to outsource so you can free up your precious time for growing your business:

- Bookkeeping and accounting
- Updating your social media profiles regularly
- Keeping your website and blog content fresh
- Shipping your products
- Sending out a newsletter
- Preparing sales documents and presentations
- Designing marketing materials
- Managing your inbox
- Responding to customer's questions and comments

Elance.com and oDesk.com are where I go to hire my virtual team members. In fact, Elance helped me find an amazing team to bring this book to fruition.

If you just have a simple task that needs to be done quickly, such as a Wordpress theme installed, a Powerpoint presentation prepared, a custom Facebook Page tab, or an intro for your videos, chances are you will be able to find someone to do it for you at Fiverr.com ◊ for just five bucks. Yes, for the price of a latté you can get someone to do just about anything for you, saving you a lot of valuable time!

I most often use Elance because I love the "workroom" feature for managing people and projects, but there are many competitive freelance sites worth checking out as well, like oDesk.com, peopleperhour.com, and Guru.com. What works for my needs may not work for *your* needs, so take these platforms for a test drive and figure out which one is best for you.

Managing a virtual team is exactly the same as managing an on-site team, with one striking difference. In the virtual world, unless you communicate via webcam, you cannot rely on body language to express an idea or interpret a response.

More essential communication is given and received through body language than through the written/spoken word. Imagine asking an employee how his work was coming on so-and-so project and receiving a "fine" with a distracted look and averted gaze. Right there a red flag would go up, warranting further investigation. With the virtual world you would take that "fine" at face value, possibly only to discover later that the project was off track.

You must set milestones and check progress frequently until a solid relationship is formed. Set deadlines and make them short at first, only releasing the leash once value and quality standards are proven. Be diligent; don't shirk your duty here and then blame employees for your lack of leadership. You will have to be much more careful to express your wishes or concerns at length to get what you want.

SEVEN TIPS AND TOOLS
FOR MANAGING YOUR VIRTUAL TEAM

When hiring a virtual team, progress will be much smoother if you keep these points in mind:

1. **HAVE A CENTRAL MANAGEMENT HUB IN PLACE.** I use Basecamp HQ ⬦ and Yammer.com ⬦ as virtual meeting places for my teams. People need to know what they are working towards, and they can view goals, overall schedule, and upcoming due dates in the hub. They can also upload documents and communicate with me, my business partner, and other members of our team.

2. **CREATE A COLLABORATIVE SCHEDULE.** Set up a Google Calendar, part of the must-have Google Apps Suite ⬦, and share it with everyone on your team. Projects run much more smoothly when your team members have some decision-making power. I always allow my team members to give feedback and collaborate, and we change gears if necessary.

3. **MAKE SURE YOU HAVE A CONTRACT.** I screwed this one up a few times, specifically with a networking website I was developing fresh out of college. Getting bitten in the butt taught me a good lesson, and I'm wiser now. On Elance I set terms and milestones that the contractor agrees to, which essentially acts as the contract. Fortunately, online platforms like oDesk and Elance take the risk out of hiring someone because they act as a mediator if there is a dispute about money.

4. **YOU HAVE TO BE WILLING TO INVEST TIME INTO TRAINING PEOPLE.** If you were hiring employees to come work at an office with you, you would train them. It's part of your business. Prepare a training

document with important information that your contractors should know about your company and their roles within it.

5. **COMMUNICATE.** Make it clear that you want to have an open line of communication for any questions or concerns, and plan at least a weekly meeting to check in and make sure everyone is on track. I do catch-up calls on Skype. For team meetings I use Meeting Burner ⬭. GoToMeeting is another option.

6. **BE A LEADER.** You have to motivate your team members and keep them happy, just as you would have to do with someone who worked in your office every day. The energy your team brings to your business can make or break you. Offer bonuses or other incentives for a job well done. Send a handwritten thank-you card. It's important to recognize hard work and build a strong team dynamic.

7. **BE SUPPORTIVE OF THE PEOPLE YOU'RE WORKING WITH.** These amazing virtual platforms like Elance and oDesk are buzzing with people who are small business owners just like you. Take the opportunity to build a relationship and recommend those who do good work. There's nothing I love more than entrepreneurs supporting entrepreneurs.

LESSONS AND CONFESSIONS:
NATALIE SISSON ON MANAGING A TEAM FROM ANYWHERE

As a Suitcase Entrepreneur, I feel very lucky to be able to take advantage of the flexible, on-demand workforce that is allowing businesses of all sizes to get more done with less. You don't need to be in the same city or country, let alone office, to have a great company and manage a top team.

I have two interns, one in Hungary and one in Japan. I also have a part-time project manager in the United States. Two were found by posting a job on Twitter. The other read my blog and offered up her hours to work alongside me.

More recently, I found a virtual assistant through HireMyMom.com. I use Elance and oDesk when I need freelance contractors for specific projects or tasks. Weekly catch-up calls are done via Skype. Project management is maintained and tracked via Basecamp, and Highrise allows us to keep on top of our customer relationship management.

Google Docs is the final overarching tool for keeping the most up-to-date documents and for working in real time.

The first hire can be the hardest, but from there it just keeps getting better! There is a kind of beauty in building an international and virtual team. The biggest factor for me is flexibility and the ability to work across borders and timezones. Essentially I have a 24/7 business.

LESSON LEARNED: *Invest in finding the best! A lot of people go for cheap contractors trying to save money, but ultimately you spend more time and money trying to train these people and get them to love your business as much as you do.*

— Natalie Sisson

Founder of The Suitcase Entrepreneur

MAP ITEM –
BUILD YOUR TEAM

LET'S BUILD YOU A POWER TEAM that can bring your MAP to fruition:

- What are the tasks you hate doing or that fall outside your core strengths?

....

....

....

....

🌍 Group tasks together that you think one person could handle. For example, circle all administrative tasks that can be completed by just one virtual assistant. Put a square around the tasks relating to your finances and accounting that can be completed by a bookkeeper or accountant.

🌍 Write a job description outlining your ideal candidate, overall vision, and what tasks the team member will be expected to complete on a regular basis.

....

....

....

....

....

....

🌍 Now, head over to Elance or oDesk, or your website of choice. Post the job, and watch people apply to work with you!

When hiring, don't forget to conduct interviews and follow the other tips given throughout this chapter.

CLOUD CHALLENGES

LIFE IN THE CLOUD, running a virtual team, is not always rainbows and butterflies. It does have its challenges. For one thing, it depends on having a good Internet connection at all times, which can be tough when you're running your business from other countries.

One day I was in Croatia and needed to get an important document sent off. With no WiFi connection and no Internet cafés open, my colleague and I started racing around looking for somewhere with an Internet connection.

You have to understand the lifestyle of people in these parts of Europe. They are laid back. Very laid back. Many people looked at us like we were crazy as they told us everything is closed because it was a holiday. I can understand stores and shops being closed for a holiday, but I thought, "This is the Internet, people neeeed Internet!" After three hours we were able to find a WiFi connection. Whew! We dodged a bullet that time.

Then in Cannes, France, for the Cannes International Film Festival, we were staying at a mobile home park that we chose specifically because it advertised wireless Internet, unlike other accommodations.

When we got there we realized that to access the WiFi we had to be on the balcony of the main office for the park. The office was far from where we were staying in the park. It was a ten minute uphill walk every time we needed the Internet. This atually wasn't bad because of all the French bread and Merlot we were enjoying, but the thing that sucked was you had to be outdoors on the balcony — not fun when it's raining and you're trying to check in on your virtual team while holding a tarp over your computer!

If you choose to take full advantage of having a virtual team by working abroad, you have to keep an open mind and learn to roll with the waves.

So running a virtual business is not without its challenges. But it's one hell of a ride and a constant learning experience. Fear not — you will discover what works best for you and your team.

CHAPTER 8

Partners and Ventures and Mentors, OH MY:

FINDING THE HELP YOU NEED TO GROW

PARTNERING UP

You know the saying, "Behind every successful man is a wise woman"? Well, *part* of my success is owed to a talented man. He's my sounding board when I'm making important decisions, my partner when it comes to world domination, and he makes me laugh when I just want to sit at my desk and scream.

Before I make him sound too perfect, I should note he contributes to my urge to scream sometimes when he breaks my productive and silent work periods by yelling "QWAAAH" and laughs hysterically as he watches me jump out of my chair, occasionally spilling coffee down my blouse.

But he's been by my side through the ups and downs of building my brand, and I adore him for it.

If you work with a male partner who isn't your spouse or your brother, people will likely question the whole male-female business partner thing, as they do with me sometimes. My business partner is gay, which makes it easy to field such questions! We actually met when he started dating my hand-some Calvin-Klein-underwear-model-lookalike neighbor.

One of the great challenges I have faced as an entrepreneur is working with business partners. Yes, at one point I vowed I would never work with a partner again, but the temptation of its benefits would always smack me in the face and bring me to my senses.

Working with a partner on your business or teaming up with someone for a joint venture can take your business to a level that you could never take it to on your own.

It took me quite some time to make all the classic partnership mistakes in business: working with a friend, working with family, even working with someone who shared the same skill set was not a good match.

Then I found Mr. Right. He's perfect for me in many ways. Our skills are complementary rather than competing, we share a strong passion for our work, he tells it like it is and he isn't afraid to ask me, "What the hell are you thinking?"

Even though all is wonderful right now, the reality is that our partnership is only 'til death — or a change of heart — do us part.

It's important to spend a lot of time getting to know your potential business partner. My partner and I had a two-year "engagement" period where we still ran different businesses, but worked together before merging and making our partnership official.

When you do make it official, you might want to think beyond just signing the dotted line. Having proper contracts in place can save you loads of time and money in the future. I sat down with Nina Kauffman, a friend and Manhattan business attorney, for some expert advice:

> *"When business owners are about to 'tie the knot' and form a company together, they lose sight of a significant fact about partnerships: the issue is not if – it's when. At some point, every partnership ends. Whether you like it or not. It may end with your leaving in a pine box (your death). It may end because your partner becomes disabled. Or has a major lifestyle change/*

change of heart. Or, it can end because you eventually can't stand the sight of each other. A business 'pre-nup' helps ensure there's an orderly transition of the business and its assets when these situations arise. When you leave these matters open (with no written agreement), you run a real risk that you won't be on the same page about buyout prices and payouts when you need to be. And that can lead to expensive and acrimonious litigation, where no one wins.

— Nina Kaufman

Founder of AskTheBusinessLawyer.com

I'm not saying you need to have a two-year "engagement" period like my partner and I had, but you should carefully consider who you are working with.

THREE QUESTIONS TO ASK YOURSELF BEFORE WORKING WITH A PARTNER

THINK LONG AND HARD about the questions below when choosing a business partner or a partner for a joint venture, so that you're absolutely sure about moving forward with the partnership:

- **WHY DO YOU WANT TO WORK WITH THIS PERSON?** Think about what he or she brings to the partnership that is of value to you.

- **WHAT WILL THE ROLE OF YOUR POTENTIAL BUSINESS PARTNER BE, AND HOW DOES IT DIFFER FROM THE ROLE YOU WILL PLAY IN THE BUSINESS?** You need someone who will share your vision, but your skill sets should be different. Write out the responsibilities each of you would have based on your skill sets. If you feel like your skill sets and responsibilities overlap too much, this probably isn't the partnership for you.

(🌙) **HOW WELL DO YOU REALLY KNOW THIS PERSON?** You wouldn't marry someone you don't know, and a business partnership is pretty much like a marriage (sans sex — I hope). Which brings me to my next point: you might also not want a business partner that you know too well or who you're sleeping with, like a spouse. If you are in business — or considering going into business — with a spouse, you should check out *Sleeping with Your Business Partner: Communications for Couples in Business Together* by the husband-wife team Dr. Becky Stewart-Gross and Dr. Mike Gross.

The glue that holds my business partner and I together is our differences. We're very different people, to the point where others don't understand how we're so close and how we work so well together. He is a talented artist with a fairly dark vision and fan base of Goths from around the world. I am on another spectrum entirely! Yet we have a harmonious yin and yang relationship that totally works for us. Find the yang to your yin, and experience an exciting and dynamic working environment.

FINDING MENTORS FOR YOUR TEAM

The final component of building a power team is summoning the experience of someone who has "been there, done that." Every successful entrepreneur I have interviewed has had a mentor who helped them get to where they wanted to be.

I have several mentors that have guided me at one point or another. More recently I have turned to Twitter to find mentors and to be a mentor to other women entrepreneurs getting started. How do you use Twitter as a hub for mentoring? It's quite simple, actually. Start by developing a short list of entrepreneurs you admire who have expertise in your industry, or in an area where you need guidance. Start engaging with one or more of them by sharing their content, re-tweeting their posts, and introducing yourself.

Once you develop a rapport, try asking the person a quick question. Once the relationship develops further, you can even ask to have a brief phone call sometime.

It's amazing how responsive people are on Twitter, and it doesn't take up a lot of time, the way formal mentoring can. Try it out! You may be surprised who steps up to the plate and offers you guidance.

LESSONS AND CONFESSIONS: MARY O'CONNOR ON REACHING OUT FOR HELP

My husband and I are not people who like to ask for help. Five years ago, at age 37, I was diagnosed with breast cancer. I thought I could get through surgery without asking for help, and I did. Then I thought I could get through chemo without asking for help, and I did. Then I broke my leg, a side effect of chemo. I was on bed rest for two weeks. I had no choice but to ask for help, and many friends and family members answered the call.

After getting dropped off at the pool with my two sons, wig on head and cast on leg, I sat down in my chair and started staring at women and the swimsuits that they wore. I noticed that some women did not wear suits at all. They opted for a t-shirt and shorts.

I decided that my new body was going to need a fabulous suit, so I created Lovely Lillies, Swimwear for Fabulously Real Women.

I knew nothing about making swimsuits, buying fabric, or selling swimwear. I was going to need a lot of help, so I told anyone who would listen to me what I was doing, and asked everyone if they had any knowledge or connections to contribute. I couldn't believe how many people wanted to help.

Then I was fortunate enough to become a member of the Tory Burch Foundation. Through this opportunity, I was connected to my first mentor, Alison Pincus, CEO of One King's Lane. She provided the guidance I needed to start my line and also connected me to invaluable resources in the industry and beyond. All of these amazing things happened because I surrendered and opened myself up to receiving help.

LESSON LEARNED: *Don't be afraid to ask for help. You may be surprised by how many people are there to lend a hand and help you grow.*

— Mary O'Connor

Founder of Lovely Lillies, LLC

DON'T FORGET THE MEN

WOMEN ARE MORE THAN CAPABLE of building thriving businesses, and more and more of us are doing just that. I love hearing about the successes of women who took the leap and became their own bosses, but I often wonder if women can achieve even more in business by partnering with or finding a mentor in a man.

I started thinking about the impact a man can have on a woman's business when I was interviewing an influential woman entrepreneur. She explained to me how one of the most successful women she knew had a male mentor with whom she worked closely. She said that women should not just seek help from other women, but from men as well. A man can offer a different perspective than that of another woman. There is obviously much to be gained from a different paradigm.

I agree with most of the value my above-mentioned interviewee verbalized. My business partner and I bring different qualities to the table when it comes to leadership, problem-solving, and brokering deals. Some of these differences are gender-based, while others are simply based on our unique strengths and weaknesses as entrepreneurs.

My partner has particularly helped me improve in two key areas: negotiation and finding focus.

I think you may find it valuable for me to take a moment here to explain my struggles with negotiating. I know I'm not the only one who has this problem. I used to make concessions on my rates when clients would ask because I wanted to be seen as the "nice girl." Now, I stand by what my value is, and if someone is not willing to pay me what I'm worth, I find another client who is.

When I try to be a multi-tasking superhero with our client work, my blog, speaking engagements and volunteer commitments, my partner is quick to bring me back to earth by encouraging me to focus. He forces me to write each task I'm working on onto a sticky note and put it on the wall, just so I can see how ridiculous my schedule is. It creates a powerful, visual representation of a scattered and overworked brain. There is no arguing with that simple kind of proof.

Having a male business partner may be a good strategic move if your company needs to raise funding as well, since the majority of venture capital is raised by men. I asked influential blogger and Brazen Careerist co-founder Penelope Trunk about the benefits of having a male business partner. In true, no-nonsense Penelope style, this is what she says:

"More than 90% of venture capital funding goes to men. We can talk all day about why that is, but instead of philosophizing, just get a male partner. Having a man and a woman on the team will get you access to the boys' club (yes, there still is one) and it'll get you access to the funds set aside for women in an effort to make inroads in that boys' club."

Does your support system consist of both women *and* men? The men in my business life have challenged me in different ways than the women have. I think it all comes back to having a well-balanced support system and surrounding yourself with people who will give you different perspectives and opinions. These opinions will help you grow your business, so weigh them all.

CHAPTER 9

Bring on the Buzz:

How to Get the World Talking About Your Brand

SALES VERSUS MARKETING

I'm often asked what the difference between sales and marketing is.

I view sales as the story, and marketing as the packaging or material with which the story is told. Sales closes the deal; marketing attracts the deal in the first place.

Sales is about the good feeling you get when you have decided to make the purchase. Marketing is what brought you through the door to begin with.

Marketing is about getting your name out there so that people know who you are. It's about associations — visual or audio, good or bad.

The other thing I'm often asked about marketing a business or brand is how to do it with little to no money. The rest of this chapter is dedicated to helping you navigate the broad scope of **online marketing** and **social media** — the most cost-effective and powerful resources for building buzz around your brand and hitting the big time. It's how I built my own brand on a shoestring budget, and it can work for you too.

There is a lot to take in throughout this chapter, so be prepared! I recommend spending some time on each section and taking notes. It will also be helpful for you to visit each of the mentioned tools and websites as you read through the sections. Visualizing the strategies will help you determine which ones will be the best fit for building your brand.

CREATING YOUR ONLINE PRESENCE

YOUR WEBSITE is perhaps the most important part of your online existence. Whether you want to build a powerful personal brand or a global enterprise, you need a rocking website that reflects your brand. Unfortunately, a lot of websites suck. There's nothing that turns me off a business more than a poorly planned, hard-to-navigate website. If you are missing any of the key points below, you're in danger of having a less-than-stellar site.

The following is a *non-negotiable,* must-have checklist for your website:

✓ **PROFESSIONAL DESIGN:** Unless you have experience designing websites, hire a designer. Again, you can find people to help you with this on websites like Elance and oDesk. A professional-looking website gives credibility to your business.

✓ **CUSTOM DOMAIN:** Your website should have a domain that you own and host. For example, mycustomdomainisawesome.com is appropriate, whereas thisisnotacustomdomain.wordpress.com would not be a suitable domain for your business.

✓ **CONTENT MANAGEMENT SYSTEM:** You have to be able to update your own website. *She Takes on the World* looks completely different than it did three years ago, and it's a good thing. If I hadn't worked on it continually and let it evolve, it never would have grown into what it is today.

I always recommend using Wordpress ◊ for your website because there are a ton of decent Wordpress developers, and it's a super easy platform to get comfortable using.

✓ **ANALYTICS:** You should know how many visitors

your website receives, where those visitors come from, and how they got to your website. Google Analytics ◊ is a free tool that gives you a comprehensive overview about your website visitors. It is what I use for my own websites and for websites I manage for my clients.

✓ **KEYWORD OPTIMIZATION:** Search engines need to be able to find your site. What do people do when they need something? They Google it. If you have the solution people are looking for, they need to be able to find you. In the copy of your website, and when writing blog posts, make sure you include keywords, phrases, and questions people would type into the search bar if they were looking for the product or service you're offering. If you are using Wordpress, install the All-in-One SEO Pack ◊ plug-in, or have your Wordpress developer or someone on Fiverr install it for you. This one plug-in increased *She Takes on the World*'s traffic from search engines by over 500 percent, and it's completely free and easy to use.

✓ **AN OPT-IN:** You need a way to keep in touch with your visitors after they leave your website. Your email list is the most valuable thing you have, especially if you want to build a business primarily online. I recommend taking a look at Aweber ◊, Mail Chimp ◊, Constant Contact, iContact, or VerticalResponse as potential platforms for managing your email list.

Now that we have rocketed through the centerpiece of your online presence, I'm going to take you through some of the best ways to build buzz around your brand.

YOU, THE CONTENT QUEEN

PUBLISHING CONTENT for your niche online is one of the best ways to establish your credibility today.

The easiest way to share your ideas, get your message across, and connect to others in your niche is through blogging. *She Takes on the World* has been the foundation upon which I built my brand. It led to dream opportunities to appear in multiple major media outlets, work with international brands on marketing to women, and become a contributor to *ForbesWoman* and *The Huffington Post.*

If the blog is for your business, it can go right on your website, or you can have a standalone blog like *She Takes on the World.* Blog updates can be distributed through what's called a "feed," eliminating the need for people to constantly visit your blog for updates. The feed sends your posts to *them.* I recommend using Feedburner 🌢 because of the data it provides you with compared to other services. It's also free!

Do not underestimate the usefulness of a blog. It is a powerful tool for building a community around your brand. It does not matter that everyone else had one first!

It's worth mentioning that a blog is a huge labor of love and it can take a lot of your time. If you don't have the time to keep it updated, you may want to write for someone else instead as a "guest author." Even I have difficulty turning out new content on a regular basis, and I'm someone with a lot to say!

Where your content is concerned, choose to create conversational blog posts that ask questions and engage your audience. Be sure to respond to comments people leave. Lists, Top 10s, and Q&As can make for great content.

The purpose of a blog is to build relationships and a community, so it should not be overly promotional. Instead, find topics to write about that will provide value to your readers.

I talk to many small business owners who tell me, "I just don't know what to write about on the blog!" It can be challenging to constantly come up with new topics and consistently write blog posts, especially when you are busy building your business. Here are ten topic ideas to get you rolling:

1. Five Things You Didn't Know About

   ....

2. Ten Quick Tips for

   ....

3. If I Had Known Then What I Know Now

4. Five Best Sites on ....

5. The Difference Between ....

   and ....

6. A Review of ....

7. An Interview With ....

8. Five Must-Read Books on

   ....

9. Seven Ways to Make Your ....

   Better

10. Four Steps to a Perfect

    ....

LESSONS AND CONFESSIONS:
CARA STEIN ON CHANGING THE GAME PLAN

I'm building a business around helping people build the lives they want and make every day count. One of my first steps was to write a free e-book to increase my mailing list and boost my social media presence.

I gave it a catchy title (How to Be Happy, No Fairy Dust or Moonbeams Required), *and poured myself into it, heart and soul. Even though it was going to be free, I wanted it to be the best thing ever.*

Finally, launch day came. I stayed up until 3 a.m. getting everything finished. I prepared for fanfare, fame, fortune, and accolades, not to mention hundreds of new subscribers.

Reality was waiting for me with a big slap. Only 13 people tried to download the book on launch day, and even they couldn't, because the link was broken.

Other than things like natural disasters and childbirth, does anything make it harder to be zen than starting a business?

The book did become a success: tons of people have downloaded it, more people know me across social media platforms now, and my subscribers increased by

750 percent in the first month and a half. But oh, the despair in the meantime!

Starting a business is awesome and horrible and scary and exhilarating. It's custom-made for nuts like me, who tend to get carried away. I wouldn't trade it for anything.

LESSON LEARNED: *When things don't go according to plan, don't give up. Rethink your plan and keep on keeping on.*

— Cara Stein

Founder of 17,000 Days

ROCKING THE SOCIAL WORLD

WHAT GOOD IS IT to create awesome content if no one is reading it? That's where social media comes in.

For now, I will stick to my fives and ask you to employ a "pick five" rule, because that's the maximum number of social networks I think you should use at a time. You can't possibly be on all of them and still be effective.

I'm going to take you through some of the main platforms I use and how to use them effectively to build your brand. What works for me may not work for you, so remember to get creative with how you use social media to build your own brand.

I also want to emphasize how quickly the social media landscape changes and evolves, and that it's not about the tools you use. It's about how you leverage social media to create a strong community around your brand.

LinkedIn

LinkedIn is like the neglected middle child of social media, with so many people focusing on Facebook and Twitter, so I'm going to shine the spotlight on LinkedIn first. This is the ultimate professional networking website for maintaining relationships with your business network and seeking new business opportunities. LinkedIn is your online resume and the place to share your experience, credentials, and career achievements with your clients and colleagues.

You should have two profiles: a personal profile and a business page. I've noticed that a lot of business owners don't have pages for their business on LinkedIn like they do on Facebook.

Make sure your profiles are completely filled in. Your profile is indexed by search engines, resulting in your LinkedIn profile likely showing up among the top search results for your name or business and generating a fair amount of traffic. For example, if someone searches for my name, "Natalie Mac-Neil," on Google, my LinkedIn profile usually shows up in the top five results. The visibility of your LinkedIn profile makes it incredibly important to keep it up-to-date.

Groups are a great way to connect with your target audience. Search for groups to join and introduce yourself to other members. Can't find the perfect group for you? Create your own group and recruit like-minded people to join.

I found that there was a need for a group that catered to readers of *She Takes on the World*, so I started the "Women Entrepreneurs and Professionals," group which has flourished into an incredible community of women.

LinkedIn Answers is a section on LinkedIn where people can ask questions of the professional LinkedIn community. As an expert in your field, you can answer questions from people in your network and extended network. This will further build your credibility, provide value to your target audience, and potentially draw in new customers for your business if you carefully choose what questions to answer and how you answer them.

FACEBOOK

Facebook is one of the most powerful social media marketing tools today and spans many demographics.

You can have a personal profile on Facebook to connect with people you *know*. Many businesses have personal profile pages for the business. A personal profile is not appropriate for your business. Your business should have a fan page, not a profile.

A Facebook fan page, with the right mix of applications, can drive traffic to your business and help you build a stronger relationship with your target audience. I recommend customizing your Facebook fan page so it doesn't look like everyone else's. Again, the easiest way to do this is by heading over to Elance or Fiverr. Get a designer to create the main image for your page to be an extension of your brand. Include important information about what your business does and how people can get in touch with you.

How Facebook really helped me catapult my business is through the Facebook Ads platform. With so many people on Facebook today, it's the perfect place to let people know about your brand and attract potential customers in your niche.

You can get very specific when you target your ads. For example, you can choose to have your ad displayed only to people who are celebrating a birthday. Why not say Happy Birthday from your brand and offer a birthday discount?

As you set the criteria for who you want to target, Facebook will let you know how many people on Facebook are within your demographic. This is also a great way to determine the approximate size of your niche market!

TWITTER

Twitter is incredible for its power to connect the world in real-time. Twitter is used for many different purposes, from keeping in touch with friends to providing customer service — even as a tool for social change, like in the case of post-election protests in Iran or the Revolution in Egypt.

Twitter is a simple platform, without all the add-on applications that LinkedIn and Facebook offer. As with your profiles and pages on other networks, you should have a consistent look and feel. You should have a custom Twitter background and a photo that is an extension of your brand.

There are two main groups on your Twitter profile: people you follow and people who follow you. Your focus should be on following people within your niche. It's all about the quality of followers you have, not the quantity!

Remember, your target audience includes potential customers as well as peers within your niche. Focus on using Twitter to build influence within your target audience by providing value to the conversation.

To find people in your target audience that are on Twitter, start by visiting Twitter directories such as WeFollow.com 🝆 and Twellow.com 🝆.

Before you start tweeting, have a plan for *what* you will tweet about. Your tweets should provide value to your target audience. People don't want to hear about what you're doing every minute of the day unless it's really interesting and relates to them.

Still not sure what you should be talking about on Twitter? These are some of the ways people and businesses are effectively using Twitter to build relationships and influence:

🐦 Tweet links to useful articles and resources for your target audience.

🐦 Ask questions to get opinions and feedback on products and services.

🐦 Use Twitter as part of your customer service platform to offer customers another channel of communication with your business. Answer questions about your products, services, and industry.

🐦 Provide offers that are exclusive to your Twitter followers.

🐦 Promote other people, products, and services you trust without getting anything in return. Your followers will come to trust your recommendations, which builds influence.

🐦 Follow-up with people who mention you or re-tweet one of your tweets. This is a great way to build more personal relationships with your target audience.

When posting links, use a URL-shortener to save space and track the number of times someone clicks your link. Bit.ly 💧 is a great url-shortener service that gives you statistics on your links, so you can measure the effectiveness of your tweets and work on improving your level of engagement.

GOOGLE+

Google+ was launched after I finished the final manuscript for this book, but I managed to sneak this section in at the last possible second before the book went to print.

Google+ allows you to create a personal profile *and* a business page. You should have a personal profile for yourself and a page for your business, just like on Facebook. Google+ allows you to organize people and brands into Circles. Circles give you an opportunity to choose who you want to share your content with. This is a valuable feature because you can choose to share personal posts only with the people closest to you, and share business-related posts only with your colleagues and clients.

Another cool feature I have been experimenting with is Hangouts. Creating a Hangout allows you to connect with your network via a video conference call. I see huge potential for using a Hangout to connect with your niche audience on a personal level. You could also use it as a customer service hub for your business. I look forward to seeing Google+ continue to roll out new features for businesses that differentiate the Google+ platform from Facebook fan pages.

HOOTSUITE

Hootsuite is something called a "client" that helps you organize and manage your social media presence on Twitter, Facebook, and other platforms.

Besides being able to schedule your content (which is an awesome feature) and manage different profiles from the same dashboard, Hootsuite allows you to track keywords being mentioned by setting up what's called a "stream."

If you set up streams to track keywords that are relevant to your business, you can respond to the needs of your target market. For example, if your business sells fabric, you can track 'fabric' and other related keywords. If someone tweets, "I'm looking for an animal print fabric," it will show up on your Hootsuite dashboard. If your fabric business has an animal print fabric, you can reply to that person with a link to the animal print fabric your business sells. Hootsuite gives you the power to meet the needs of your target market in real-time.

YouTube

YouTube is the second largest search engine in the world (Google is number one). If you develop video content, you can share it on YouTube to reach an enormous-sized audience.

Creating videos is a good way to share knowledge, put a face on your brand, and build awareness. Businesses can use YouTube as an educational tool to provide video tutorials on how to use a product or service.

Creating an interesting video that appeals to your target audience could potentially go viral. This is a term you have probably heard. It means the video is shared across multiple websites and platforms. For example, a great company called Grasshopper made an animated video, *Entrepreneurs Can Change the World,* as part of a marketing campaign to rebrand its services. The video captured the hearts of entrepreneurs everywhere and it brought Grasshopper a lot of attention.

If you don't have a video camera, the Flip Camcorder or Kodak zi8 are popular choices for beginners. For professional quality video, you can always post a job on Elance.com if you think it would be a valuable marketing tool for your target audience.

StumbleUpon

I'm going to let you in on a little secret that helped me build a large audience for *She Takes on the World* within a few months of launching. The secret is StumbleUpon.

StumbleUpon is essentially a recommendation engine that shows users web pages that target their profile preferences. Users have the option of rating the web page with a "thumbs up" if they like it or a "thumbs down" if they don't. A user's favorite web pages get displayed on her StumbleUpon blog, which gets shared with her network.

Participating in the StumbleUpon community and actively sharing articles and commenting on other people's posts can definitely get more eyes on your website. It can take some time to build up your network on StumbleUpon, though, so have patience.

What makes StumbleUpon so valuable to small businesses is its affordable advertising platform, StumbleUpon Paid Discovery ⬮. You can choose the gender, geographic location, interests, and age range of the people to whom you want your web page displayed. This will bring you targeted traffic at an affordable price.

You have to sign up for this service at stumbleupon.com/ads; it is separate from the regular StumbleUpon network.

When you start a campaign, you can set a daily budget and choose from three different advertising options starting at just five cents per unique visitor. Throughout the campaign you can see how many people give your content a "thumbs up" or a "thumbs down." I recommend setting up a few different campaigns with different parameters to evaluate which campaigns give you the most "thumbs up" reactions.

BUILDING A THRIVING COMMUNITY

AFTER ALL THE RESEARCH, planning and listening, it is finally time to start talking and building relationships — the latter being the most important. Building meaningful relationships and a sense of community needs to be the main reason that you use social media. Yes, social media can also bring you more customers and increase your revenue, but that will only happen *after* you build genuine relationships with people and gain their trust.

Let's look at a company everyone knows: Starbucks. Starbucks is ranked the most socially engaged brand by the Engagementdb Report.[4]

I chose Starbucks as an example not because they are the most socially engaged brand, but rather because the social media strategy Starbucks uses can be used by any business, big or small.

Starbucks has over 17,000 stores and over 128,000 employees. With that kind of global reach, guess how many people are on the Starbucks social media team?

The answer is six. That's right, only six people (at the time I'm writing this book) are responsible for all of Starbucks' social media activities and the brand's own social network. If that doesn't get you excited about the fact that it is realistic for that you to build a social media presence as good as that of Starbucks, I don't know what will!

Starbucks also understands how to use different engagement strategies, depending on the social media platform being used. For example, Starbucks uses its Facebook fan page to collect ideas from fans while providing a platform for them to come together and discuss their love of coffee and the Starbucks brand.

In contrast, Starbucks uses Twitter to respond to customer questions, offer customer support, and release news.

Starbucks kicked off its social media strategy with the launch of MyStarbucksIdea.com, a crowdsourcing website for customers to share ideas they would like Starbucks to implement.

Crowdsourcing is a popular trend that gives customers some power to solve problems and make decisions for a company.

All ideas submitted to My Starbucks Idea are read by Starbucks and voted on by other Starbucks fans. People can also track the ideas that are being implemented. My Starbucks Idea shows that Starbucks values its raving fans and their ideas, while building upon the strong relationship Starbucks already has with its customers.

Building your own network, like Starbucks did with the launch of My Starbucks Idea, is the ultimate community builder.

As someone who has built a custom social network from the ground up, I will tell you that it definitely has its challenges and requires a lot of resources. The good news is there are websites that allow you to easily create your own social network for free, or at a very low cost.

Ning.com ⬥ is the most popular platform for creating your own social network. It also happens to be co-founded by my friend and a powerhouse woman tech entrepreneur, Gina Bianchini. It only takes a few minutes to have your network up and running, and there are many options for customizing the network to be consistent with your brand image.

SocialGo is an alternative to Ning, and CrowdVine ⬥ is a good option for building a community around an event or conference.

Focus on strengthening the relationship between your brand and your customers, as well as building relationships between your customers to create a community. Sales through social media will come only after you have developed these relationships.

Get to it and have patience.

GETTING IT TOGETHER

HAVING OFFERED MY TOP TIPS about websites, blogs, tools, and strategies, I'm now going to now take you through how I put it all together to build my global brand.

I think one of the best things I did early on with my blog was to have it professionally designed. Please, please, please hire a designer instead of using a generic template! The design really made *She Takes on the World* stand out from the millions of other blogs out there. I invested money into marketing and promoting *She Takes on the World* at the same time. I knew that even though it wasn't making money when I started, I would have to invest in growing it if I wanted it to be a leading website for women entrepreneurs. I guest-blogged and connected with a lot of other bloggers at the start as well.

It was tough in the beginning. I remember in 2007 when I had something like forty readers. While you're small, encourage people to contact you and focus on building relationships. This helped me build solid relationships that have benefitted me greatly.

One of the biggest mistakes I made was not building my email list sooner, however. I would've been even further ahead if my newsletter was set up from the get-go. Aweber is the newsletter service I use and I love it. I must admit that it's not as user-friendly as some of the other email marketing services, but the data it gives you is killer.

Twitter has been amazing for me as well. It's a huge investment of time and you have to be patient, but it can be pure gold for your business.

I used tools like WeFollow.com and Twellow.com to find relevant people in my niche to start following when I first joined Twitter.

In the beginning I looked for:

- ❦ **POTENTIAL CUSTOMERS**

- ❦ **INFLUENCERS**

- ❦ **MY PEERS**

When Twitter's "Lists" feature was first introduced, I quickly created lists to sort people and keep tabs on those who consistently tweet great content. My Lists are where I find most of the content I re-tweet.

I used Hootsuite to monitor keywords like women entrepreneurs, women in business, etc. which allowed me to participate in the larger conversations out there. I also connected a lot of people! I wrote one of the original "Women to Follow on Twitter" lists for *Forbes*.com, and it connected and promoted some fabulous women, many of whom I still have solid relationships with myself.

Whatever you do, DO NOT talk about what you're doing all day. Use Twitter to recommend people and resources, share valuable information, and re-tweet other great content.

It's easy to get caught up with reading people's tweets for good chunks of the day, so make sure you set limits on your usage. I check Twitter in the morning and usually only once more during the day. I start my day by using StumbleUpon to find content that my audience would enjoy. I'll tweet a piece of content and then use Hootsuite to schedule other great content, which gets posted while I'm working throughout the day.

Then there's Facebook. I started my fan page late, and that was a mistake. I should've had it much sooner, although when I first started blogging, Facebook was very different than it is now. Your business definitely needs a Facebook page, and your personal brand could benefit from one too. I use the fan page to share *She Takes on the World* content and content from other women's business sites. I "like" other relevant pages and regularly connect and participate in conversations.

The best advice I have on this is to share, share, share. A lot of people ask me if they really need both Facebook and Twitter. I say yes! To me, Twitter is like mingling at a cocktail party, whereas Facebook is like going for a coffee with a friend. Short and sweet conversations for Twitter; longer, engaging conversations on Facebook.

Another main part of my strategy is LinkedIn. I have connected with a lot of people in my niche, and I started the group "Women Entrepreneurs and Professionals" which is a great community of women on LinkedIn. Feel free to go over there and introduce yourself to our growing community of women in business.

Last, you want to bounce people around to your different pages, profiles, and networks. Offer different resources and things to do on each unique platform; try to keep people engaged in your community.

I can't stress how important it was for me to use social media to LISTEN, rather than talk, as I was growing my brand. I carefully track mentions of my name and brand through Google Alerts 💧 and SocialMention.com 💧 which allows me to listen to my audience and their needs. After all, it's about them. They are why I do what I do.

This is my personal strategy and there is no one-size-fits-all solution here. Also, in this industry, things are constantly changing and evolving. In fact, by the time you read this book you may be thinking, "Natalie, what about (insert name of latest and greatest social media platform here) that you forgot to mention?" In the time it took to get this book published, the whole social media landscape may have changed. Let me say this again, though:

IT'S NOT ABOUT THE TOOLS WE USE TO GROW OUR BRANDS. IT'S ABOUT BUILDING A COMMUNITY THAT MAKES PEOPLE FEEL LIKE THEY'RE HOME.

Never lose sight of that.

CHAPTER 10

Juggling It All:

HOW TO MAKE WORK
WORK FOR YOU

GOODBYE BALANCE

Like many endeavors, juggling is its own art form. If you concentrate on all the flying objects at once, they will certainly all fall into a disorganized heap at your feet. But as you learn to release, catch, release again, and catch again, you can achieve a zen-like rhythm amidst the constant movement.

I'm speaking of something quite different from multitasking. In fact, I believe multitasking can sometimes hinder your ability to accomplish a smooth toss, and limit you to far less than your true capacities might allow.

Enter the concept of "strategic imbalance."[7]

In a moment of extreme imbalance, I found myself hungrily turning the pages of a fantastic book by Marcus Buckingham called *Find Your Strongest Life* (Thomas Nelson, 2009). I had been drawn to his work by an article he had written in *The Huffington Post,* and I credit his work to one of my a-ha moments, where the twisted vines of the universe suddenly spelled out a truth that had been right in front of me the whole time.

In a moment of quiet reflection, the concept of *strategic imbalance* bloomed before my eyes and energized me to make a change.

There is a beautiful concept in the Buddhist religion that speaks of balance. It has permeated our culture and is well on its way to becoming a prolific meme. The idea that all unhappiness is caused by unfulfilled desire and imbalance seems so simplistic until you try it out on your own life.

I would think, "Okay, I'm out of balance is all. I should reassess what I'm doing and give everything equal attention."

This would seem like a brilliant idea until I tried it.

I would attempt in vain to add equal amounts of time and importance to each area of my life, only to find myself dreading the day's tasks. I had to try extremely hard to follow the "balanced regimen" that I had prescribed for myself. I felt out of sync and not at all myself.

"Wow, being in balance is really hard!" I would think before reverting back to my slightly chaotic, million-tasks-a-day, familiar self. I was obviously comfortable with being uncomfortable. Could this be true?

What my a-ha moment revealed is that balance, like beauty, is in the eye of the beholder. *Balanced* does not necessarily mean *even*. *My* balanced state is an individual state of being, and is unique to me.

Your balanced state will serve you best if it fits into your mold, not someone else's.

Here again, for the second time in my life, I was learning that following other people's paths would never work for me. I had to develop my own path, as tempting as trying someone else's solution might seem.

So how do you figure out balance on your own terms? Simply put:

LEARN TO SAY NO, LEARN WHAT IS TRULY IMPORTANT, AND TAKE TIME FOR YOURSELF.

We women often drive ourselves crazy trying to smash the pieces of life's jigsaw puzzle into a vision of what others see as happiness and success. As you may have already figured out, that doesn't work.

To create your own happiness and success, you must focus and make choices. You can do it all eventually, just not all at the same time.

"MAKING TIME"

MY FRIEND MARYBETH has a jam-packed life. She is enthusiastic, energetic and poised to become a powerful force in the world of architecture. Being naturally creative, inventive, and good at math, she has excelled in her field.

At times, hearing about her frustrations with a lack of personal time and missed family moments struck a familiar chord in me. I became curious about how she manages her time and what she does when she feels stretched thin.

"I eventually just decide to make the time," she laughed.

Here was that familiar phrase, "making time."

Why do we hear this phrase repeated so often by those of us who are considered to be successful? What does it really mean? Surely we cannot create more time out of thin air. Something else must be going on.

This is where purposeful imbalance rescues us with its answer. Stop doing what is less important and do something truly important instead.

LESSONS AND CONFESSIONS:
CAROLINE CENIZA-LEVINE
ON SAYING "NO"

My business is four years old right now, and while we've had growth from year one, it is only now that I am close to replacing my corporate salary. I contribute half of our household income, so my business needs to support my family.

The financial pressure is significant, and at one point in the early days of my business, I received an unexpected offer to return to corporate life in a big role for a well-known company — at a higher salary than I had ever made.

It was really scary, but I turned down the job. Soon after, I brought in several of my biggest contracts to date.

LESSON LEARNED: *We women entrepreneurs are such doers, but sometimes saying "no" is the most important thing you can do.*

— Caroline Ceniza-Levine

President of SixFigureStart LLC

FIVE WAYS TO BETTER MANAGE YOUR TIME

You may not be able to "make" time but you sure can manage it.

1. **PRIORITIZE WHAT'S IMPORTANT.** This seems simple enough, but it requires careful thought. What is important comes from what you value. Many people value family and relationships, as an example. I'm sure you can agree that peace of mind, solitude and physical health are important to you as well; therefore, you value personal time.

   Your values ARE YOUR LIFE. They are the reasons you get up in the morning and why you work so damn hard. Finding your values and making them a priority will cause your schedule to conform to your life and not the other way around. Manage your time. Run your schedule or it will run you!

2. **LEARN TO LIFESOURCE.** Just like we have to outsource work to a team in our businesses, we can do the same in our lives. Can someone else do your housework? Can you pay someone to run errands for you? Hire a virtual assistant to pay your bills. Manage your time by making your money work FOR you.

3. **DON'T BE AFRAID TO SAY NO.** Are you saying YES when you should be saying NO? Saying yes can feel great in the moment, but we often end up resenting our commitments or continually backing out of them when we could have avoided this with a simple "No." Live with less resentment and feel the power of integrity as you commit with confidence to the people in your life.

4. **TAKE TIME-OUTS WHEN NECESSARY.** There are times when I can't focus on ANYTHING, I start

wasting time, and I feel my energy drain. When that happens, there is no point in continuing to sit in front of a computer screen. I know I won't get anything done. So I get up and get moving, or spend some time doing a guided meditation to refocus.

5. **REMEMBER THAT YOU ARE THE MOST IMPORTANT PERSON IN YOUR LIFE.** This one is hard for many women, as they place such a high value on relationships and the happiness of others. Why do we devalue our own bodies and personal time, sacrificing our most perfect moments and opportunities for a leg up in our endeavors? It's truly not worth it in the end. How can a half-functioning mind or a broken body bring joy to those around us? It can't. It only brings worry and pain. Choose to value yourself — mind, body and soul — as you would a child, and you will see the true, transformative beauty of self-love.

MAP ITEM –
CREATE YOUR ULTIMATE SCHEDULE

ANOTHER COMPONENT of my MAP is an outline of the routine I try to follow. It's time to create your own routine that fits around your life:

Redesign your schedule by carefully considering the following questions:

⚲ **WHAT HOURS ARE YOU ABLE TO DO YOUR BEST WORK?** Many of us perform best at particular times of the day. When have you always known you were likely to be "on the ball?"

🐦 **WHAT HOURS DO YOU NEED OPEN FOR OTHER THINGS?** Where are you always running around like a crazed woman, making excuses and possibly swearing to yourself? Find that troublesome time crunch and change it. Move things around and make it right! Sometimes, relieving yourself of that one-hour problem can make the other 23 hours seem like a breeze.

🐦 **PEN "YOU TIME" INTO YOUR SCHEDULE.** Block off time for exercise, reading, quiet reflection, getting together with friends, and other activities that bring you joy. One of the best things I ever did was schedule an hour for myself in the morning for a jog, yoga, a big glass of green juice, and meditation. It literally changed my life.

🐦 **WHAT ARE YOU ABLE TO OUTSOURCE?** Write down the tasks you would outsource if you had unlimited funds. Put these in the order of most importance, first to last.

Take the top three and endeavor to explore the actual cost today of outsourcing these activities. Take that total cost per month and divide it into days. What can you get for $5 dollars a day? $10? $20? How close does this number come to an hour's worth of your work each day?

Does it seem worth it to spend that one half-hour or hour's pay to NOT have to do those tasks yourself?

How happy do you feel when you think about NOT having to do these tasks yourself?

Make a plan and make it happen!

	MON	TUE	WED
7 AM			
8 AM			
9 AM			
10 AM			
11 AM			
NOON			
1 PM			
2 PM			
3 PM			
4 PM			
5 PM			
6 PM			
7 PM			
8 PM			
9 PM			
10 PM			
11 PM			
MIDNIGHT			

	THU	FRI	SAT	SUN
7 AM				
8 AM				
9 AM				
10 AM				
11 AM				
NOON				
1 PM				
2 PM				
3 PM				
4 PM				
5 PM				
6 PM				
7 PM				
8 PM				
9 PM				
10 PM				
11 PM				
MIDNIGHT				

CHAPTER 11

Women on Top:

MOVING MOUNTAINS AND SHAPING A BETTER WORLD

STANDING ON COMMON GROUND

NOTHING MAKES ME MORE HOPEFUL than thinking about a world with more women entrepreneurs and the kind of change we can create if we work together. We are now a more powerful force than ever, and if we can find enough common ground to band together, we are going to shake up the economy and change the world.

There is power in numbers, and the more of us there are, voices loud and in unison, the faster and more powerful the waves of change will be.

Women, by nature, invest more in communities, are more philanthropic — and, arguably, are often better-equipped leaders than our male counterparts. If we can help each other find ways to better manage our careers, money and time, there will be no stopping us.

Why do some people say that we make better leaders? The answer may be found by understanding the role women have historically had as nurturers. We are natural family leaders. We have been running households, managing different personality types, and energizing people to common causes for centuries.

These innate skills and transformational leadership qualities reverberate into the business world with widespread effectiveness. Just how different could the world be with more women running companies, organizations, and even countries? Let's take a look.

TRANSFORMING THE WORKPLACE

How many times have we heard that a company is only as strong as its weakest link? Companies are dependent on their people to make the right choices, and people depend on the relationships around them for support and growth.

A system with an archaic set of rules — "do as I say," rules, perhaps — will fail when pitted against a company that is value-driven. Value-driven companies bring their people together and create new ideas and brain spaces, allowing for rapid change and growth. They are, in a word, *adaptable.* These are the kinds of companies women may be especially adept at creating.

This kind of flexibility in a company beats out rigidity and power plays. Older models of thinking may pass down ideas like "aim for a competitor's weak spot" or "crush the competition." Like water, women tend to simply move around rigid thinking and obstacles, looking for the easiest path to success.

In a fantastic article by Linda Lowen, a simple concept is illuminated: women are better persuaders.[5] We're not talking about classical, logical debates here; we're talking about the power of listening, empathy and making people feel heard.

How many times have we urged our brothers, husbands, sons and male friends to just listen? Two minutes of listening can mean the difference between dissension in a business or a harmonious workplace.

Complaints can be gifts, after all. If you hear a common problem, it's easy enough to fix with a single action most of the time.

Do not underestimate your inherent gift of persuasion. Like language, women have been developing this gift for as long as they have walked the earth. Being considered the "weaker" of the sexes for so long has given us quite a long time to hone the skills we possess today.

The difference between manipulation for one's own cause and ethical persuasion for the betterment of a group is a line women seem to dance across better than men. Understanding values and how to navigate the unfeeling corporate landscape with ethics is where women truly shine.

Persuading people to merely give a radical new idea a chance would be one example of ethical persuasion.

Helping people feel personally vested in a cause breeds more loyalty than chest-beating or any number of threats. It's that power of persuasion stemming from love that so easily trumps fear.

BREAKING THE RULES

THAT LEADS US TO ANOTHER AREA in which women excel. We aren't afraid to break the rules of business as usual. In "Why Women Make Better Leaders Than Men," Ronald E. Riggio explains how women encourage "out of the box" thinking and reward that behavior, which tests the less trodden paths in life.[6]

We tend to be less exposed to traditional methods of problem solving. This lack of indoctrination to current belief systems regarding how leadership is supposed to look and act is what gives us a decided edge over our male counterparts. We are less apt to respond with knee-jerk reactions to difficult situations, and can view problems with fresh perspectives.

Adversity is another area in which Lowen notes we easily rise above, specifically when it comes to rejection. Women are far less inclined to fall in line and obey than they are to dig in deeper to prove themselves. This is a powerful leadership skill. Where others may tend to grumble and sulk at rejection, women tend to move around these obstacles to eventually demonstrate their ideas as valid.

This can cause much confusion and turover in companies that elect to hire sharp business women. The expression of these skills and gifts can seem like disobedience to male counterparts, and feminine leadership may be disdained by more traditional men.

This often leads women to search for companies that will value their input. Or they become their own bosses — which is, of course, my path of preference for strong women everywhere.

AN ARMY OF WOMEN ENTREPRENEURS

I TRULY BELIEVE that women are in the best position we have ever been in. We have been groomed for generations to take leadership roles with grace and confidence. Every system has a cycle and it is our time to make our mark.

I'm not at all saying that women are better than men. I simply believe that the power structure is changing, and this change is a welcome one. We could use more philanthropists and healers. Women give to social causes and charities more than men and we volunteer our time more freely as well. We are poised to change the very face of the planet — and not a moment too soon.

We spent ages hammering, stomping, and throwing rocks at the glass ceiling — to great effect. Really, take a look at the new world around you. It *has* changed. Get to know the powerful women that make up your global community. Find what you have in common and help each other towards those goals.

A powerful principle that guides my business, and my life, is this:

**WHAT WE GIVE TO SOMEONE ELSE —
BE IT TIME OR LOVE OR AN OPPORTUNITY —
WE RECEIVE BACK IN ABUNDANCE.**

What we imagine, we create.

Imagine creating bonds and relationships with the powerful role models out there today. When they give of their time, knowledge and support, they are planting seeds for those very gifts to return to them many times over. Women empowering women is the smartest way we can help each other thrive and succeed.

Give often, never compromise your values, and connect often with your fellow women entrepreneurs. Value yourself and know yourself. Potential is fantastic, but realizing that potential is when you have become a success. Allow those around you to be objective mirrors for you, and don't get lost in the forest.

Above all, love who you are and what you do. It's your life, your MAP, your creation — so go for making a masterpiece!

MAP ITEM –
CONNECT THE DOTS

MY LAST ACTION ITEM for you is to reflect on all the elements of your MAP often and keep a personal journal as you continue the journey of being your own boss, working happy, and living on purpose. These are some of the things you should keep track of:

- What you are grateful for

- People you meet

- Opportunities that have come your way

- Lessons you're learning

- Experiences and "coincidences" that feel like they were meant to be

- What your inner voice is telling you

The amazing thing about doing this is that you can go back and connect the dots. You'll start noticing that your life is a beautifully spun, interconnected web. I can't even count how many times I've reflected on the journal entries I keep as part of my MAP and then sat in astonishment as I connected the dots. When you connect the dots in your own life, you can also serve others by offering connections and opportunities.

WE TAKE ON THE WORLD

THE WORLD ISN'T MERELY CHANGING — it has changed already. Smart business needs a MAP, partners, and careful execution. Smart women examine their values, write a plan according to those values, and stick to it no matter what — because it is a reflection of your passion and your very being.

TO GO AGAINST YOUR PASSION AND PURPOSE IS TO WORK AGAINST YOURSELF.

Define yourself, lose the fear, and lead. Realize the immense power and purpose you have inside *you*. And get comfortable with it.

When I interviewed Barbara Corcoran, she said something to me that stuck. It was something her mother had told her when she was young: "You have the right to be here."

You are exactly where you are supposed to be, and don't forget it.

Don't just guess, KNOW. Know your strengths, know your weaknesses, know your best match and KNOW YOU CAN DO IT.

Magnetize other strong women to you by exuding passion through your every pore. Help others and receive the help you need in return.

Let's step into our power and use it to create change. Let's lead a Sheconomy that values people, relationships, and the planet. Let's use our businesses to improve our communities and support important social causes. Together we can move mountains.

There are opportunities waiting at every corner. The world needs you. I have just one question left:

Are you ready to take on the world?

She Takes on the World:

MINI-GUIDE AND Q&A

THE MINI-GUIDE

THIS MINI-GUIDE summarizing key sections of the book is for you to return to whenever you need guidance, inspiration, or a kick in the butt.

- Look at your MAP every day. Do not assume you remember every facet. Know why you are looking at it. Make evaluations often. Be vigilant and adaptive. Meditate on your vision and stay focused on the bigger picture.

- Learn to say no. Women can take on way too much and capsize under the weight. I have done this. I have been at that point so many times. It is a struggle to change, but it is worth it. If you feel like you're drowning, consult your plan and make the necessary cuts to discard the excess weight. It is never someone else's fault. Take responsibility for your failures as well as your success and you will have done well.

- Consider a partner wisely. It's a big decision, so really think it through. Consider even more carefully when deciding to partner with a spouse, friend, or family member. Don't partner with another you! Find someone with different skill sets than you, and play to each other's strengths.

- Always keep a strong team around you. You are not using your time wisely if you think that you need to do every little thing yourself. Work on generating revenue and delegate other tasks to employees and partners.

- 🐦 People buy good stories, not products or services. Take time to develop a good story and educate your customers, drawing them in with the history and benefits. Remember to listen. Strive to understand what people really want and sell them that idea.

- 🐦 Take advantage of the Internet and social marketing. Not having an online presence today is like not having a business sign or a business card to offer. Make connections often and reach out to your customers. At the click of a button, there are thousands of tutorial videos to walk you through any social network process with which you are unfamiliar.

- 🐦 Let your MAP guide your schedule and activities, and evaluate your opportunities. Decide whether an opportunity is worth it or not by asking yourself if it is in line with your carefully crafted plan. Will it meet the needs of your niche? If you create a tool and forget to use it, what good can it possibly do?

Q&A

AFTER NEARLY FOUR YEARS of running the blog, coaching entrepreneurs, and building my own business, I've answered countless questions people have at every stage of running a business. I put some of the top questions into this handy section for you. Many are already answered throughout the book. However, I wanted to make sure there was a section for you to get quick answers to the challenges you're facing.

Q: Natalie, I have a lot of different interests, but I feel like I haven't discovered my one true passion yet. Help!

A: Not everyone has "one true passion" and that's okay as long as the work you're doing falls into the range of things you're passionate about. If your inner voice is telling you there's something better for you or you should be doing something else, you should listen. Turn to page 36 for a list of questions to consider when searching for your passion.

Q: What's a niche and why do I need one?

A: A niche is a group of people with a common passion, interest, or pain who need what you are offering. A niche has to be specific, but not so specific that there won't be enough customers to buy what you're offering. You need a niche because you can't be everything to everyone. You need a niche to focus your content, marketing efforts, products, and services towards to be successful. Turn to page 42 to determine what the best niche is for you to focus on.

Q: What is "working happy?" I want that!

A: Working happy means you are 1) following your passion and living on purpose, and 2) working no more than absolutely necessary. Working no more than necessary doesn't mean you're lazy or lack dedication. It means you hire help or outsource the "work" part of your business (usually the tedious tasks that drain you, or the areas in which you have weaknesses). The work you're good at and love doing usually doesn't feel like work! Play to your strengths. Do the tasks you're best at, focus on working on and not in your business, and hire help for what feels like "work"—that's the foundation of working happy.

Q: I'm afraid to start a business because my income might drop, I don't know how to market myself, I don't understand social media, or (insert other reason here).

A: Those sound like a lot of excuses to me! I know how tough it is to build a business, but do you know what's tougher? Watching someone else successfully turn your idea into a business. I have a little ritual I do when I need to release fear-based thoughts. I take out a piece of paper and cut it into pieces. On each piece, I write down a fear. If it pops into my head I write it down—no filtering. Then I burn each piece of paper one by one, letting my fears leave my mind and go up in smoke. I'm sure your local fire department thinks that's a bad idea, so you can also tear the piece of paper to shreds instead.

Q: I love that you incorporate mantras and meditation into your business and working life! What are the top three mantras you recommend for entrepreneurs?

A: Yes, meditation and mantras are part of how I stay focused in my business and everyday life. Here are three of my favorite mantras that I have on sticky notes where I can see them often:

- ⟐ I am attracting new opportunities that allow me to do what I love.

- ⟐ Today I am one step closer to achieving

  ....

- ⟐ I am becoming wealthier every day that I follow my passion and honor my purpose.

There are more on page 60, so check those out too!

Q: What is your goal setting and business planning process?

A: Every year I write a Bigger Picture Strategy as part of my MAP. It combines goal setting, strategic planning, and vision boarding. I set five major goals with five strategic actions and milestones for each one. I look at my Bigger Picture Strategy almost every day of the year, and let it guide my daily actions and to-do lists. Want to create your own Bigger Picture Strategy? I take you through the full process on page 86.

Q: I can't afford to hire a team right now, but I'm feeling really stressed out because I run my business all by myself.

A: Actually, if that's the case, you can't afford not to hire a team. If you continue the way you're going, the stress will only build and lead you to resent your business. The concept of hiring help when you feel you aren't generating enough revenue is a difficult one to grasp, but it is essential to earning the income you dream of earning. You'd be surprised how affordable it is to hire help, which I talk more about on page 112. Having a team will free up your time for important tasks like bringing in more clients to increase your revenue. You can't do that when your head is buried in paperwork and administrative tasks!

Q: Do I really need an email list? Isn't that just one more thing I'm going to have to spend time on?

A: Yes, you really need an email list. Your website, blog, social media profiles are all ways in which your potential customers come to you. Your email list is your way of getting to them! Your list is how you communicate with your community. Email marketing software like Aweber, Mail Chimp, and iContact make it easy to send out a newsletter or email blasts when you have exciting news or a special offer.

Q: I don't know what to blog about! Help!

A: Yes, it's hard to produce great content month after month, year after year. For some topic ideas, check out page 139.

Q: I'm on social media, but how do I develop a strategy for getting results?

I hear this a lot; you're not alone! I know it can be confusing, and many people find it frustrating because social media evolves so quickly that it can be tough to keep up. Social media is the backbone of my business and has allowed me to create a flourishing career in an unprecedented amount of time, so I'm a huge advocate for sticking with it and figuring out what works best for you! I go through my personal strategies beginning on page 141.

Q: *I'm having a hard time creating balance in my life with a business, a family, and so many other commitments!*

A: Personally, I don't believe in "balance," and I think as women we stress ourselves out way too much trying to achieve it! Let go of the concept of keeping everything in perfect equilibrium and breathe a sigh of relief. We often place ourselves below everyone else, and when we do, we lose our ability to truly live on purpose. How can a half-functioning mind or a weak, exhausted body bring joy to those around us? It can't. To give the world the best of you, you need to give yourself all the love and energy you give others. For more tips on managing your time, visit page 161.

Q: *Do I need a business plan if I'm starting a business?*

A: In short, no, unless you're raising funding or need a huge loan to start your business. You do need a plan, you just don't need a plan that's packed full of bullshit that you'll never look at again after creating it. When launching a new business or product I like to do a Compass (the Compass). It's short and sweet and helps you consider some important questions that you should be able to answer before you start anything. Check out page 87 for the Compass outline.

Q: *Natalie, are you a man hater?*

A: Absolutely not! I love men and I am blessed to have amazing men in my life who believe in the power of women to change the world. My father always told me that women should run the world! I'm not saying we should run the world, but we make up over half the world's population and what I really want to see is that ratio reflected in our businesses, organizations, and governments. We need the support of men to make that happen, and men are ALWAYS welcome into the *She Takes on the World* community.

WHAT'S NEXT?

THIS IS JUST THE BEGINNING of your journey and our movement. Here are five ways you can stay connected to our community and help share our message with women around the world:

1. Start by visiting http://www.shetakesontheworld. net/backstagepass to access your exclusive bonuses, watch videos, share your story, and more

2. Post a review on Amazon.com and on your blog or website

3. Connect with me on Twitter @nataliemacneil

4. "Like" the Facebook page at http://www.facebook. com/shetakesontheworld

5. Share the book with 5 women you know who are taking on the world

NATALIE'S GEMS

HERE IS A LIST of my favorite tools, books, websites, and other fantastic resources that are discussed throughout the book:

Marketing Yourself and Your Business

- Aweber.com
- Facebook Ads
- Google Adwords Keyword Tool
- MailChimp.com
- StumbleUpon.com/ads
- SurveyMonkey.com

Managing Your Online Presence

- All-in-One SEO Pack Plug-in for Wordpress
- Feedburner.com
- Google.com/Alerts
- Google.com/Analytics
- SocialMention.com
- Wordpress

Social Media Beyond the Big Networks

- Bit.ly
- CrowdVine.com
- Hootsuite.com

- Ning.com
- Twellow.com
- WeFollow.com

Managing a Virtual Team

- BasecampHQ.com
- Elance.com
- Fiverr.com
- Google Apps Suite
- MeetingBurner.com
- oDesk.com
- Yammer.com

Books

- *Spirit Junkie,* Gabrielle Bernstein
- *The Four Hour Workweek,* Timothy Ferris
- *Think and Grow Rich,* Napoleon Hill

Money Matters

- inDinero.com
- Kickstarter.com
- Shoeboxed.com

Giving Back

◊ Kiva.org

◊ ShesTheFirst.org

◊ WhiteRibbonAlliance.org

WORKS CITED

1 Emergent Research, Intuit, Inc., and Institute for the Future. *The Intuit 2020 Report.* Rep. Intuit, Inc., 12 Oct. 2010. Web. <http://intuit.com/2020>.

2 *Women Small Business Owners Will Create 5+ Million New Jobs by 2018, Transforming the Workplace for Millions of Americans.* Rep. The Guardian Life Small Business Research Institute, Dec. 2009. Web. <http://www.smallbizdom.com/research/index.htm>.

3 Hagel III, John, Johny Seely Brown, Duleesha Kulasooriya, and Dan Elbert. *The 2010 Shift Index: Measuring the Forces of Long-Term Change.* Rep. Deloitte Center for the Edge. Web. <http://www.deloitte.com/us/2010shiftindex>.

4 Engagementdb. Web. <http://www.engagementdb.com/downloads/ENGAGEMENTdb_Report_2009.pdf>.

5 Lowen, Linda. "Qualities of Women Leaders." Weblog post. *About.com.* The New York Times Company. Web. <http://womensissues.about.com/od/intheworkplace/a/WomenLeaders.htm>.

6 Riggion, Ph.D., Ronald E. "Why Women Make Better Leaders Than Men." Weblog post. *Psychology Today.* 9 Mar. 2010. Web. 15 Aug. 2011. <http://www.psychologytoday.com/blog/cutting-edge-leadership/201003/why-women-make-better-leaders-men>.

7 Buckingham, Marcus. *Find Your Strongest Life: What the Happiest and Most Successful Women Do Differently.* Nashville, TN: Thomas Nelson, 2009.

ACKNOWLEDGEMENTS

THIS BOOK HAS BEEN A LABOR of love for the last two-and-a-half years of my life. I'm incredibly excited to give it wings and let it soar, and I am overflowing with gratitude for the people who helped make it happen.

In this book I emphasize the importance of building a great team and publishing a book requires that you have a phenomenal support system of people who believe in the book as much as you do.

I'd like to start by thanking a few people who got me past the finish line on this extraordinary project.

Behind most every successful writer is a great editor. Stephanie Monty, my valued first-pass editor, helped me focus and organize what I wanted to say. Robyn Landis, my insightful senior editor, polished the book into the professional and expressive gem I had envisioned, bringing clarity and strength to my words from the big picture down to every last comma.

People may say "never judge a book by its cover," but the cover is the first thing people see so it's hard not to! I want to thank my creative partner, Vincent Marcone, who designed the cover of my dreams. Thank you to Kevin Hansen, the amazing photographer behind the cover photo, and Gabriela Soares, who did my hair and makeup to complete the look. The jacket and interior design was done by the talented Stasia Blanco. Thank you for bringing my vision to fruition!

I offer gratitude to Wendy Lazear and the team at Infinity Publishing for bringing my vision to fruition. Thank you to Manisha Thakor who first encouraged and guided me to bring my message to the world. To Cindy Ratzlaff, I appreciate your honest feedback and insights into the world of publishing.

To all the women who contributed their stories for this book, thank you for sharing your journeys with me. To my business partners, Vincent and Natalie, thank you for being on this crazy ride with me and for pushing and pulling at just the right times.

Last but not least, I wouldn't be where I am today without my family — all of you know who you are, and I love you all so much. Thank you to my mom and dad for your unwavering support as I follow my dreams and take on the world. To my aunt and uncle who inspired me to start my own business, thank you for nurturing my entrepreneurial spirit.

Octavian, thank you for supporting me through the ups and downs of building my business and personal brand. And gratitude to the Hall family for lending me their beautiful cottage in the final days of writing, so I could have a peaceful place to unplug and finish the journey of writing my first book.

I also want to acknowledge all of the amazing women — and men! — who may use the messages and tools I offer here to grow their passions into successful businesses that make our world a better place. I applaud you for your courage, vision, and commitment.

ABOUT THE AUTHOR

Natalie MacNeil is an EMMY Award-winning media entrepreneur, influential blogger, and thought leader in the sphere of entrepreneurship and leadership for women.

Natalie is best known as the Founder and Editor-in-Chief of *She Takes on the World*, which received international attention when it was listed by *Forbes* in "Top 10 Entrepreneurial Sites for Women." It is also the 2010 winner of Blog of the Year at the Stevie Awards for Women in Business.

Natalie is a contributor to *ForbesWoman* and *The Huffington Post*. She is frequently quoted and interviewed by the media discussing women and entrepreneurship, branding, and new media. She has appeared in several media outlets including *Forbes.com, ForbesWoman, Wall Street Journal, Entrepreneur.com, Mashable, Examiner.com, Financial Post, TechVibes, MSN, AOL, and CNN.*

In 2010, Natalie was named Canada's Young Entrepreneur of the Year by the Impact Organization. She graduated with an honors degree in Political Science and Business from the University of Waterloo in Ontario, Canada, where she currently resides.